container
gardening

PAUL WILLIAMS

container
gardening

London, New York, Munich, Melbourne, Delhi

Project editor	Bella Pringle
Project art director	Robin Rout
Set design	John Crummay
Set building	John Crummay & Robin Rout
	Gone Wild Ltd
Senior managing editor	Anna Kruger
Senior managing art editor	Lee Griffiths
Senior art editor	Alison Donovan
DTP design	Louise Waller
Production controller	Heather Hughes

First American Edition, 2004

Published in the United States by
DK Publishing, Inc.
375 Hudson Street
New York, New York 10014

04 05 06 07 08 10 9 8 7 6 5 4 3 2 1

A Cataloging-in-Publication record
for this book is available from the
Library of Congress.

ISBN 0-7566-0372-2

Color reproduction by Media
Development Printing Ltd., UK

Printed and bound in Slovakia
by Tlaciarne BB s.r.o.

Discover more at
www.dk.com

Contents

container
introduction

Introduction

Container gardening is both a craft and an art.

It is a way of growing plants that can be very satisfying to gardeners. In pots, the plants are seen close up, and this gives us the incentive to nurture and cultivate them to a high standard. And because of the portable, contained nature of the plantings, it allows us to grow plants in our gardens that might otherwise be impossible to cultivate because of unsuitable soil or climatic conditions. Container gardening feeds the artist within us because it allows our imaginations the freedom to combine plants of all colors, shapes, and textures, to match the plants to the pot, and then to place the container display where it does the most to enhance the garden.

It is this combination of the practical and the aesthetic that makes container gardening the most exciting and versatile form of gardening. No matter what your budget, the scale of your garden, or your level of skill or aspiration, you can create a planting that is an expression of your personal taste, a planting that reflects your love of color or texture, a planting that gives cheer in the gloomiest parts of the garden, and you can grow plants in areas where no soil exists—for example, on a balcony or roof terrace.

Bearing in mind that it can honestly be said that any plant can be grown in a pot, the almost unlimited range of plants in the container gardener's palette could be considered daunting. Or you could see it as an opportunity to explore and experiment with any number of combinations of color and texture; a chance to mix the soft with the hard, the bright with the subdued. This diversity of plant material means that every taste and style can be catered to, from the tightest formal look to the wildest informal display. Whether you wish to make a statement or simply want some pots that look pretty on the patio, there are pots and plants available to do it with, and to do it with style.

Top left There has never been such a choice of pots available. Choosing a "special" pot is all part of the pleasure and skill of gardening with containers.

Top right How does this look? Matching plant to pot, checking scale and proportion, blending colors and textures: these are just a few of the artistic decisions to make when putting together a container display.

Bottom left Abundant plantings like this one thrive when given plenty of care and attention. Take pride in deadheading flowers regularly and pruning straggly stems, and you will be rewarded with beautiful results.

Bottom right Even routine chores, like watering, can be enjoyable. I use this opportunity in the evening to mentally relax after a hard day and to check the health of the plants.

On the following pages, I have brought together a range of plants that I have found useful for creating a wide range of effects. I have grown them all. Some are traditional plants like Lobelias and Impatiens; others, such as Plectranthus, are more unusual and have been chosen in the hope that they will encourage you to search out and experiment with new species. Some plants are hardy and some tender; many can be found at a good garden center and others will be harder to track down; but all provide a distinct color or texture useful in putting together a planting.

I like to compare the skill and the art involved in creating a container planting to that of flower arranging. Most of us have at some time placed a few flowers in a vase and enjoyed the results. Some of us have taken a little bit more time and arranged the flowers so that they show themselves off to best advantage. A smaller number of us really go to town on flower arranging and are always on the lookout for new flowers or foliage and unusual vases and vessels. There is a lesson to be learned from the dedicated flower arrangers, and I think gardeners could do worse than borrow some of their energy and ideas. But the flower arrangers have an easy time compared to the container gardener. They have the advantage of be able to place their arrangements out of the way of strong winds, baking sun, and drenching rain. Florists can always work happily in the knowledge that what they arrange will stay pretty much the same for the life of the display.

The container gardener—with a few exceptions—has to have a vision of how the display will look several months later, when the planting matures. The few small plants planted at the beginning of the season are going to grow, and by the end of the summer, there will be a container burgeoning with flowers and leaves. In the meantime, you have had to water, feed, prune, and pinch out as well as do battle with the pests and diseases that do their best to thwart your efforts. It is not off-putting; it is gardening.

Top left Gardening is all about plants, and to be able to grow so many, so well, in such a confined space, is thrilling to the gardener.

Top right Container gardening gives you the opportunity to study, close up, details of flowers and foliage that might otherwise go unnoticed.

Bottom left In the confines of a container, the contribution each leaf shape or flower makes becomes an important element in the overall design.

Bottom right Both hardy and tender plants make up the very broad palette of plant species that grow successfully in containers.

container
design

Color

Container gardening gives you the opportunity to be very specific in your choice and use of color.

Plants in pots are in intimate contact with each other, and their area of display is confined. So in container plantings, the subtle color details and combinations that might easily become lost in a border setting are there to be appreciated, right in front of you.

If you are unsure about how to use color in your plantings, take inspiration from lifestyle and interiors magazines and translate what you find there into ideas for plant and container colors. And try the following color combinations, which I find work well. White is extremely versatile: with green it achieves a unique freshness; with yellow and green it is cool and lively; with pinks and blues it has a romantic feel; and it really sets off bright colors such as oranges and reds.

Purple works in many combinations: with gray and pink it is sophisticated; with yellow, more light-hearted; with brown it is somber but classy; with crimson it can appear regal; with orange, jazzy; and with white, cool. Blue as a flower color is in short supply, but any element of blue in a planting is eye-catching. Reds, yellows, and oranges are ideal for flamboyant displays; with magenta and violet they make vivacious mixes.

Color is a useful tool for creating different moods. Gray-blue Elymus and Festuca grasses and plum Heuchera leaves, matched up with pale gray terrazzo planters and galvanized metal, create a cool, contemporary feel. Here, the success of the display relies as much on texture and tone as on color.

Combinations using just one plant and pot color in all the containers are an easy and direct way to produce a purposeful display. Here, traditional terracotta and a molded resin "studded" pot have been used in combination with fiery orange Isoplexis and Cuphea to create a Mediterranean-style terrace.

Limiting the planting plan to just one or two colors is by far the easiest way to give your containers a designed look. By planning out the color palette in this way, the whole display becomes more focused and unified. Here, purple Salvias, magenta Tibouchina and magenta and white Impatiens have been chosen to create the desired color effect.

There are times when you want out-and-out exuberance, and this is best achieved using a riotous mix of colors where no rules apply. Make maximum use of the container color and look for plant material in bright and contrasting hues. Here a vibrant display is achieved by growing one-color and one-species plantings together to give you the flexibility to switch between different styles.

Texture

The sole aim of ornamental gardening is to excite the senses and bring us pleasure.

Plants with textural foliage not only stimulate us visually, but also invite us to get up close and touch them. Inevitably, you will want to feel or caress their leaves to see if they are as smooth, silky, rough, hard, soft, or spiky as they look. The opportunity to experience pleasurable tactile sensations is definitely one of the joys of gardening.

As a container gardener, you can work with the range and interplay of textures by putting together plants with a similar feel, such as those with soft and furry leaves and stems, or those that are fleshy and smooth. You can also develop interesting contrasts of texture by planting the hard and smooth next to the soft and velvety. Through the textures of the plantings that you use within a given space, different moods and effects can be created. Sharp, spiky plants make for a lively and energetic atmosphere, while softer, more pliable plants induce a more relaxed and mellow feel. These principles apply not only to foliage but also to flowering plants. And always remember to include the container in the equation. Select a material or a finish that will enhance your textural planting and produce a distinctive display.

The artistic gardener has to be resourceful and remember that not only the color but the texture of the plant material can produce fabulous results. This simple two-plant combination could be quite ordinary but for the energy supplied by the grasses' wispy, untamed appearance. Their tangled mass makes you want to comb your hands through the strands and caress the soft seedheads.

There are a few instances where one plant offers a perfect blend of all the features of texture, color, and balance we are trying to create with a mix of plants. The Japanese painted fern (Athyrium niponicum var. pictum), shown here, combines all the attributes I could wish for—a sophisticated, harmonious pink, gray, and green color theme, a balanced shape, and a soft, interesting texture.

In the plant world, texture, color, and shape are closely linked, since many plant characteristics have developed together in response to environmental factors. Here, the straplike leaves of Phormium have a shiny surface and are set against the matt finish of the cast-iron container. Though these details of texture are small, without them, the effect of this planting would be diminished.

Plantings that rely solely on texture have a sophistication that is hard to beat. I enjoy them because the display is carried by the distinctive character of the leaves. Here, I have used two extremes of leaf size and texture. The large Kalanchoe leaves are furry and could not be more different from the feathery foliage of Lotus maculatus and L. berthelotti and the speckled, fleshy pennies of trailing Cerapegia.

Scale and proportion

Getting these two important design elements right is one of the greatest challenges of container gardening.

The proportions of every planting are constantly changing as plants grow and mature. This certainly presents a problem for container gardeners, who must try to see the finished display in their mind's eye when planting: a difficult task when young plants, at this stage, may be less than a quarter of their eventual size.

When planning the scale and proportion of a display, it is important to consider the growth habits of the species you have chosen; this will help you figure out how the planting will look over time.

For standard designs, which feature a tall central plant in a round pot, the finished height should ideally be between one and one-and-a-half times the height of the container, and the planting roughly triangular in shape. But this proportion of container to planting is not a rigid rule to be applied in every instance. When you look through the chapter on Container Portraits *(see pages 26-115)*, you will see that it is a flexible guideline to be adapted according to the shape of the container. Generally, I try to avoid large plantings in pots with narrow bases because they upset the eye by appearing top-heavy, while the same plants in a wide-based pot look stable and pleasing.

Traditional container planting designs use a tall plant in the center to balance the pot height and to create a focus for the display. With smaller, rounded pots, it is best to avoid height in the center since it makes low arrangements look top-heavy. Instead, create a dome-shaped design that can be enjoyed from all angles. Here, *Tradescantia* and *Ageratum* work to make a well-balanced planting.

This low-level planting of *Echeveria* takes a significant but secondary role, allowing the pot's large size and rounded shape to dominate the design. Its smooth, curved shape is accentuated by this low surface planting of succulent leaves. This choice of planting helps to keep the whole display's center of gravity low and creates an overall effect of stability, security, and solidity.

These two very different pot sizes and shapes sit against their own wall but work well together. The choice of plants and the clever play on scale help accentuate the shape of the pots, but I would prefer the grass to be shorter and the *Agave* bigger for balance.

Balance tall, narrow pots with tall plants that are at least twice the height of the pot. Ideal subjects include the grasses Molinia caerulea *subsp.* arundinacea 'Bergfreund' *and varieties of* Miscanthus sinensis, *which offer height, grace, and a lightness that does not challenge the weight of the pot. Alternatively, choose a broad and full plant that does not grow above half the height of the pot to balance the proportions. Here, I have used the hardy* Fuchsia magellanica 'Versicolor'. *Trailing plants visually reduce the scale of tall pots, but use them with a tall companion plant for best effect.*

Shape

Careful use of shape can help to create drama and excitement, or calmness and serenity.

The most obvious expression of shape in the container garden is topiary, where plants are clipped into geometric or fanciful shapes for effect. Less manicured expressions of shape, however, can be achieved by using plants with large or distinctive leaves or imposing arrangements of branches and stems. These "architectural" plants often work best when used on their own in containers, rather than as a mixed group, so that their shape really stands out. Indeed, a single well-shaped plant can have sufficient presence to stand alone as the centerpiece of a small courtyard or patio garden.

When grown in containers, plants such as *Mahonia japonica*, *Aralia elata* 'Variegata', Aucuba, Yucca, Cordyline, Phormium, *Acer palmatum* 'Dissectum', *Rhus glabra*, *Fatsia japonica*, and many palms and bamboos offer a wide range of foliage and shapes to enhance a garden design. Effective on their own as garden focal points, they also work well as the main feature in a larger group of pots.

When relying on plant shapes to create impact, avoid unduly fussy pots, since the detail will detract from the main theme. Pots with simple outlines and strong shapes will work much better.

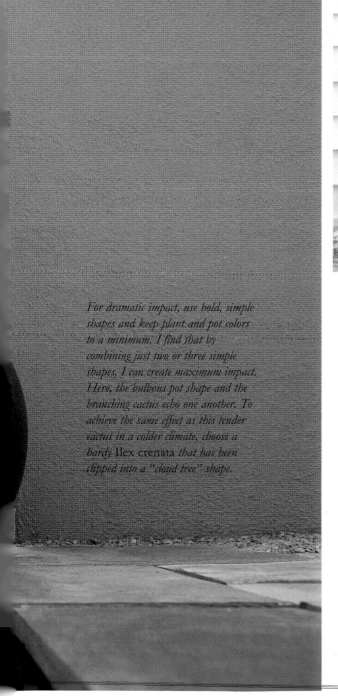

For dramatic impact, use bold, simple shapes and keep plant and pot colors to a minimum. I find that by combining just two or three simple shapes, I can create maximum impact. Here, the bulbous pot shape and the branching cactus echo one another. To achieve the same effect as this tender cactus in a colder climate, choose a hardy Ilex crenata *that has been clipped into a "cloud tree" shape.*

Plants that rely on shape and structure rather than flowers for their effect are of great value to the container gardener when creating simple, modern displays. They are most effective when used in uncluttered surroundings with few other visual distractions.

In my experience, curved lines and rounded shapes in the garden create a more relaxed, informal atmosphere and promote feelings of calm. I like to use curved handmade pot shapes, as shown here, in conjunction with willowy plants like bamboo or the smaller, arching leaves of grasses, such as Stipa arundinacea, S. tenuissima, *and* Hakonechloa macra *to engender this atmosphere of tranquility.*

Shape can be used to create different moods within a garden space. Here, the shape of this finely balanced stainless-steel container creates a mood of fragility and instability as it sits on its pointed end. The spreading nature of the plants further exaggerates the balancing act. Squat, dumpy shapes create the exact opposite effect—that of solidity and assuredness.

Repetition

In the container garden, repeating patterns and symmetry please the eye and comfort the mind.

Repetition and symmetry are design elements that are fundamental to most of the great gardens with their avenues of trees, balustrades, steps, topiary, and knot gardens. Seeing a single component repeated over and over again does instill a feeling of abundance and prosperity. Rows of large potted orange trees flanking a walkway, for example, are an impressive sight. While most of us cannot emulate the scale of grand designs, we can apply the idea to our own, more modest gardens, to create a sense of largesse and comfort. Even on a small scale, identical repeated plantings engender admiration and convey a suggestion of wealth. Rows of pots can also be used to emphasize or exaggerate perspective along a path or a walkway, and you can transform an ordinary rise of three or four garden steps into a grand entrance by placing an identical pot at either end of each step. Repeated plantings can be incorporated among the plants in a border. Use large containers that stand above the existing planting and place them along the length to create continuity and give the border coherence. Harmonizing the container planting with the border either by color or style will also enhance the overall effect.

By using the same pots and plants in a row, the design takes on a formal, almost regimental precision. The pots are tall enough to act as a barrier and can be used to mark off areas of the garden and help define the space. I like to think of them as traffic cones! When placed alongside a path, a row of identical pots can even make an ordinary walkway appear quite special.

Plantings do not have to be large for repeated patterns and themes to be effective. Small displays can be placed on a garden table, on outdoor shelving, in alcoves, or on windowsills to be appreciated both indoors and out.

Here, repetition is treated in a slightly different way. The same pot and plant materials are repeated, but the container and plant shapes are different. Boxwood topiary in ball shapes and spirals is planted in terrazzo containers of different shapes and sizes. A mirror effect adds to the repetition of the design as the pots sit in front of a reflective stainless-steel surface.

This row of identical pots filled with hardy, abundant plantings transforms a plain paved yard and will last throughout the year. Each pot is planted with Heuchera, Stipa arundinacea, *and* Carex *'Evergold'.*

Grouping

Moving pots around, trying them this way, trying them that way, is one of the joys of container gardening.

With careful positioning, a group of disparate pots can be built into a cohesive arrangement that has far greater impact than the sum of the individual pots.

Grouping pots together is a great opportunity to make the most of their varying heights and styles. The other advantage of groups is that any gaps created by less mature plantings can be successfully disguised through skillful placing and overlapping.

In creating container groupings, you are combining the principles of balance, shape, and proportion that you have already applied to an individual planting. A group arrangement also has more potential, giving you the flexibility to constantly rearrange the individual pots for maximum effect.

As the plants start to grow taller and begin to fill out, move the pots apart slightly to give each planting the chance to develop fully and to create a more sumptuous display.

To add variety of height to your grouping, consider raising some of the pots on other upturned pots or standing them on shelves. This is particularly useful for smaller pots, making them more visible and increasing their stature.

Successful color and texture effects can be quickly achieved by bringing together groups of pots containing different plant species. This method is ideal for combinations of plants where one of the species might only look its best for a few weeks. When a plant is at its peak, quickly maneuver it into place next to a complementary planting for maximum effect.

By grouping plants from a similar habitat or climate, you can recreate the essence of that environment. Here, a large vine is placed alongside an olive tree. Pots of lavender, rosemary, and other sun-loving plants could also be introduced to recreate a warm, dry, Mediterranean-style garden.

Placing pots and plantings of similar style and color together can engender a specific mood within a given part of the garden. Here, a white stone urn, a terracotta pot, and the use of delicate foliage and pink flowers, such as Pelargoniums, creates a country-style feeling of freshness and cool.

Small pots like these can be easily moved and rearranged as plants come into flower and then fade. By growing only one type of plant in each pot, there is huge scope to keep reorganizing the group to create the best combination of height, color, and texture. A tableau like this can be constantly refreshed.

container
portraits

Sunset shape

If I had to choose one leaf or flower color above all others for container gardening, it would be purple.

INGREDIENTS	QTY
Agastache 'Apricot Sprite'	× 4
Cordyline australis Purpurea Group	× 1
Lavandula 'Fathead'	× 2

In my view, purple is invaluable to the gardener. It is a very versatile color with the ability to harmonize with almost all flowers and foliage. Many plant species are available in purple tones, and these offer an unimaginable variety of textures and shapes to add interest to container plantings. Here, the smooth, shiny, eggplant-colored pot is set against matt purple Cordyline leaves, while a band of soft gray Agastache foliage and apricot Agastache flowers act as a go-between—delicious. In the background, the bumblebee heads of the French lavender (*Lavandula* 'Fathead') make a subtle link between the shiny plum pot and the softer purple Cordyline foliage.

Agastache 'Apricot Sprite'   See p.158

PLANTING DETAILS

Planting plan No clever planning here. The Cordyline goes in the center of the pot, and the four Agastaches are planted around it, leaving space for the two Lavenders on either side at the back. Bear in mind that Cordyline leaves can vary in color from purple to brown. This one has distinctly purple leaves, and I think it is worth the effort of tracking down a good purple color form.

Plant care Technically speaking, this planting should be classified as tender, but if kept in a warm, sheltered site, the Cordyline and Lavender will live through the winter in many areas, while the Agastache will die back and shoot again in spring.

Cordyline australis Purpurea Group   See p.165

CONTAINER DETAILS

Style and **Shape** The glazed ceramic pot has a rich eggplant color and a considerable size, which gives it a strong presence in the garden. When viewed from standing height, the planting, and particularly the dense Cordyline in the center, appears more in balance with the pot size. With a large, cylindrical container, try to achieve a planting at least as high as the pot is deep to maintain good proportions.

Size Height 21 in (53 cm); Diameter 18 in (45 cm).

Material Frostproof glazed ceramic.

Lavandula 'Fathead'   See p.172

Scarlet and black

Color has a powerful impact. Here, deep flower and foliage colors create a wonderful, moody display.

INGREDIENTS	QTY
Dahlia 'Roxy'	× 3
Pelargonium 'Harvard'	× 4
Persicaria microcephala 'Red Dragon'	× 1
Rhodochiton atrosanguineus	× 1
Sambucus nigra 'Black Lace'	× 1

There are many ways of displaying this sophisticated container planting to best effect outdoors. Its strong, dark color palette will create a dramatic statement when set against a flower border of deep purple-red Peonies, dark blue Delphiniums, or the drooping flower spikes of *Buddleia* 'Black Knight'. This deep-colored planting can also be used in an area of the garden where flowers and foliage, or even the hard landscaping, reflect more light into the planting to bring the darker flower and foliage colors into sharp relief.

Dahlia 'Roxy' See p.166

Pelargonium 'Harvard' See p.176

PLANTING DETAILS

Planting plan This is one of my favorite color plantings but for one item; the yellow centers of the Dahlia flowers upset the carefully planned color balance. Pedantic? Maybe. The rest of the planting is a moody blend of purples and reds with lightening touches of fresh green provided by the Pelargonium leaves, while the feathery Sambucus foliage at the back balances the heavier Dahlia foliage decorating the front. The Sambucus also provides physical support for the more delicate Rhodochiton stems, while the Persicaria pokes its strong shoots through it all.

Plant care If the Persicaria leaves get too rampant, pinch out their growing tips.

Persicaria microcephala 'Red Dragon' See p.177

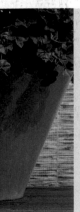

CONTAINER DETAILS

Style and **Shape** I like this pot. A broad top and narrow base give it a funnel-like shape, which you might think is unstable, but its base is wide enough to make it stand firm. The funnel shape allows for plenty of front-to-back depth in the planting as well as providing room for a large volume of potting mix so that the plants grow strong and healthy.

Size Height 20 in (50 cm); Diameter 24 in (60 cm).

Material Galvanized steel.

Rhodochiton atrosanguineus See p.180

sambucus nigra 'Black Lace'   See p.180

Modern black

Black on white is the ultimate in monochromatic contrast and produces a very startling modern effect.

INGREDIENTS	QTY
Aeonium 'Zwartkop'	× 1
Ipomoea batatas 'Blackie'	× 3
Ophiopogon planiscapus 'Nigrescens'	× 5

Black and white is a classic design combination, and I thought it would be an exciting challenge to reproduce this color theme with plants. White flowers come with green leaves and stems—which I didn't want—so instead I decided to get my pure, unadulterated white from the pot surface while relying on plants with black leaves and stems to do the rest. But black also posed a problem because I'm not convinced that any plant really is true black. Though many varieties are labeled as "black," most are just very dark shades of purple or red, as is the case with Aeonium and Ipomoea. However, I do think *Ophiopogon planiscapus* 'Nigrescens' is the best "black" there is in the plant world for container gardening.

Aeonium 'Zwartkop'   See p.158

PLANTING DETAILS

Planting plan Having decided on using just "black" plants, I could almost say that this display chose itself because of the very limited choice of large plant subjects available in this color. *Aeonium* 'Zwartkop' was an automatic choice for its height and shape. *O. planiscapus* 'Nigrescens' had to be included because of its depth of blackness. The non-climbing Ipomoea was chosen for its wonderful leaf shape and deep, deep color. When positioning this planting, remember that the whiter the surroundings, the darker the foliage will appear.
Plant care Plenty of sunshine will keep the plant foliage at its blackest.

Ipomoea batatas 'Blackie'   See p.171

CONTAINER DETAILS

Style and **Shape** I decided to use a pot that was pure white but had a rough texture to give it some warmth. I thought that a marble-smooth white surface would have made the whole display look too cold and clinical. This container planting is small enough in scale to sit on a modern garden table or, for even greater effect, in an alcove in a white stucco wall.
Size Height 12 in (30 cm); Diameter 16 in (40 cm).
Material White stone composite.

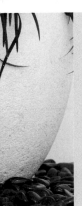

Ophiopogon planiscapus 'Nigrescens'   See p.174

Light and shade

Few flowers are to be seen in winter, so strong leaf shapes are important for year-round plantings.

INGREDIENTS	QTY
Heuchera 'Can-Can'	× 3
Juncus effusus f. *spiralis*	× 1
Teucrium scorodonia 'Crispum'	× 3

This dark plum and fresh green planting satisfies the need for texture, shape, and color in the garden during the winter months by successfully mixing the evergreen foliage of three hardy plants. The pale green, crinkled-edged leaves of Teucrium act as a foil for the dark plum-veined leaves of Heuchera, while the twisted Juncus stems fire out from the heart of the planting with vitality and humor.

In summer, this planting earns its place in the garden by providing a shade-tolerant mix of flowers and foliage. I find that shady corners are often neglected during the summer and look bare during the winter when the rest of the garden is dormant. This effective planting offers a good year-round solution.

Heuchera 'Can-Can' See p.171

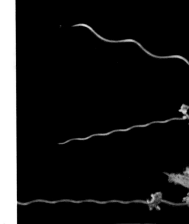

PLANTING DETAILS

Planting plan The *Juncus effusus* f. *spiralis* forms the central plant in this design and is planted in the middle of the pot. The Heucheras and Teucriums are then planted alternately around the edge of the container.

Plant care Plants sited in shady corners are often overhung by trees or shrubs and so are sheltered from the rain and may dry out. Do not forget to water them. *Teucrium scorodonia* 'Crispum' is a rambling plant that will need trimming to prevent it from engulfing its neighbors. In sheltered spots, the Heuchera will produce vertical spires of flowers for several months; these look good set against the curly Juncus stems.

Juncus effusus f. *spiralis* See p.172

CONTAINER DETAILS

Style and **Shape** This low container is intended for a site at the top of a flight of garden steps so that it can be seen as you walk up or down. Alternatively, place it close to a favorite garden ornament or sculpture. The display will add some heartening greenery throughout the winter months in milder regions.

Size Height 16 in (40 cm); Diameter 20 in (50 cm).

Material Handmade frostproof terracotta.

Teucrium scorodonia 'Crispum' See p.182

Cool and fresh

Simple colors and clean lines create a refreshing blend. This planting makes good use of both.

INGREDIENTS	QTY
Chlorophytum comosum 'Variegatum'	× 3
Cordyline australis	× 1
Cuphea hyssopifolia 'Alba'	× 3
Impatiens 'Accent White'	× 6
Plectranthus madagascariensis	× 4

Taking inspiration from the pure white pot, the structure of this planting is simple as is the color—just greens and whites. *Cordyline australis* must surely have been designed for the container gardener; take a pot, place a Cordyline in the middle, and you are halfway there.

The only other consideration is what to put around it. To avoid a stark effect, the swordlike leaves need a balancing softness. Here, I have used a variegated Plectranthus that arches gracefully as it flows out of the pot but is substantial enough to balance the strong shape of the Cordyline. This combination works in sun or shade but is at its best where its lightness can lift a shady area.

Chlorophytum comosum 'Variegatum' See p.165

Cordyline australis See p.164

PLANTING DETAILS

Planting plan Tucked in among the Plectranthus is a mix of frothy white Cuphea and large, glistening white Impatiens. To stop the Cuphea and Impatiens from becoming an amorphous jumble, there are three plants of the very common variegated Chlorophytum spiking their way through, echoing the shape of the Cordyline leaves.

Plant care Deadhead Impatiens regularly, and remove any split or discolored stems from the Chlorophytum as they age.

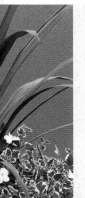

Cuphea hyssopifolia 'Alba' See p.166

CONTAINER DETAILS

Style and **Shape** This smooth terrazzo pot has a marblelike coolness that is given an extra chill by its white coloring. I have used soothing, complementary greens, but you could also try bright contrasting colors. To balance the pot and planting, the Cordyline was chosen to be at least as tall as the pot is deep. The broad base of the pot gives it a stable look, but it still retains some elegance, and it can hold plenty of potting mix—very important when relying on foliage for effect.

Size Height 24 in (60 cm); Diameter 24 in (60 cm).

Material White terrazzo.

Impatiens 'Accent White' See p.170

Plectranthus madagascariensis See p.179

Rampaging reds

United by a well-planned color theme, hardy shrubs and tender perennials will mix happily.

INGREDIENTS	QTY
Euonymus fortunei 'Emerald 'n' Gold'	× 1
Petunia 'Trailing Red'	× 3
Sambucus nigra 'Black Lace'	× 1
Solenostemon 'Midnight'	× 1
Verbena 'Aztec Red Trailing'	× 3

Hardy plants have different characters and needs from tender plants, and sometimes these are so different that it seems strange to find them alongside one another in a mixed planting. It is a clash that is hard to explain, and perhaps one only noticed by experienced gardeners who are familiar with the hardiness of their plants and realize when they make uneasy bedfellows. Here, two very different hardy shrubs are successfully combined with tender plants using an overall color theme to bring all the elements—pot included—together. The lacy Sambucus leaves add a wispy topping to balance the full red skirt of Petunia and Verbena flowers.

Euonymus fortunei 'Emerald 'n' Gold'   See p.168

Petunia 'Trailing Red'   See p.179

PLANTING DETAILS

Planting plan Neither the Euonymus nor Sambucus is going to get much bigger during one growing season, so choose sufficiently large plants to start with. Choose a Sambucus as tall as the pot is deep. Plant these two main elements first, with the variegated Euonymus in the middle of the pot in front of the Sambucus. Position the Solenostemon in front of the Euonymus, then fill in with Petunias and Verbenas. I like to use variegated foliage like Euonymus in pots because I think their unnatural-looking leaf color and slightly exotic nature are of benefit in container plantings while making them difficult to reconcile in a garden planting.
Plant care The Petunias and Verbena need regular deadheading.

Sambucus nigra 'Black Lace'   See p.180

CONTAINER DETAILS

Style and **Shape** The pot has a high-shine finish that almost defies outdoor use. I have used vibrant reds to draw attention away from its high-gloss finish while using darker Solenostemon leaf color in the middle and top of the planting to spread and diffuse a depth of color through the whole arrangement.
Size Height 18 in (45 cm); Width 18 in (45 cm).
Material Black glazed ceramic.

Solenostemon 'Midnight'   See p.182

Verbena 'Aztec Red Trailing'   See p.185

Sculptural shapes

Single, stand-alone elements can be brought together to create a stunning group for far-reaching impact.

INGREDIENTS *left container*	QTY
Phormium hybrid	× 1
INGREDIENTS *center container*	QTY
Solenostemon 'Winter Sun'	× 1
INGREDIENTS *right container*	QTY
Canna 'Durban'	× 1

Any one of these planted pots looks balanced and stylish on its own, but bring them together and they have an impact that is far greater than they would have individually. The colors and shapes of the plants and containers have been carefully selected to harmonize and bring a balance to the whole. Grouping containers provides an opportunity to play with height, scale and proportion, color, and shape. By giving thought to the juxtaposition of pots and plants, a collection of ordinary-looking plantings can be turned into an arrangement that makes a statement not just about itself but about you and your skills as an accomplished container gardener.

Canna 'Durban' See p.163

PLANTING DETAILS

Planting plan These rusty iron containers share a common style, but each planting has been carefully thought out to complement its neighbors' leaf shape and character, while a contemporary warm orange color theme links the vibrant, leafy foliage in all three pots and the rusty iron containers.

Plant care These are all sun-loving plants. The Canna and Solenostemon benefit from being sheltered from the wind. Wind protection will prevent the large leaves of the Canna from becoming ragged and ensure that the slightly brittle branches of the Solenostemon do not snap off as the plant grows.

Phormium hybrid See p.178

CONTAINER DETAILS

Style and **Shape** These tall planters are hollow to reduce their weight, but they are still robust and well-balanced. Each pot has a smaller square metal box welded inside, and these have sufficient space for one plant to grow well, which suits their simple style. The interest is created by the way the pots are grouped.

Size Height 44 in (110 cm); Width 20 in (50 cm) *(large planter)*.
Height 40 in (100 cm); Width 16 in (40 cm) *(medium planter)*.
Height 28 in (70 cm); Width 20 in (50 cm) *(small planter)*.
Material Rusty iron.

Solenostemon 'Winter Sun' See p.183

Shimmering silvers

Despite its ability to tolerate the hottest sunshine,
this gleaming silver display presents an icy coolness.

INGREDIENTS	QTY
Convolvulus cneorum	× 3
Leymus arenarius	× 3
Silene uniflora 'Swan Lake'	× 2

Plants with gray or silver leaves offer a clear signal to the gardener that a species is tolerant of hot and dry conditions. Here, two graceful and charming white-flowered plants, Convolvulus and Silene, grow alongside Leymus, a strikingly colored and fast-growing grass. Though only 20 in (50 cm) square, the gleaming white terrazzo container looks very substantial and illustrates the solid, "settled" effect that can be achieved using straight-sided planters. This display looks good set in a sleek, minimalist garden setting but also in the midst of lush greenery, where the white and silver flower and foliage colors will stand out from the background.

Convolvulus cneorum See p.164

PLANTING DETAILS

Planting plan This is a front-facing display, so the tall grasses are planted along the back edge of the container, while the Convolvulus occupies the middle, and the Silene is planted at the front of the pot so that it can trail over the edge.

Plant care This is a hardy perennial planting that would last for many years if it wasn't for the fact that Leymus is very invasive, and, given the chance, will take over the whole pot in one or two seasons. To prevent this, break up the planting at the end of the season, take out most of the Leymus, and remake the display. I also cut off the Leymus flowers early before they turn brown.

Leymus arenarius See p.173

CONTAINER DETAILS

Style and **Shape** Square pots allow for a large volume of potting mix and offer plenty of space for plant growth. Here, there is room for the Leymus grass to run around before it starts to overwhelm the other plants. While the grass is growing to its full height, the design appears to be bottom-heavy. To help redress this imbalance, I have planted a frill of dangling *Silene uniflora* 'Swan Lake', whose white, tutulike flowers help interrupt the massive scale of the pot.

Size Height 20 in (50 cm); Width 20 in (50 cm).

Material White terrazzo.

Silene uniflora 'Swan Lake' See p.181

Abundant style

A busy plant mix creates a floriferous display with a cascade of white flowers through the season.

INGREDIENTS	QTY
Abutilon 'Nabob'	× 1
Helichrysum petiolare	× 2
Helichrysum petiolare 'Limelight'	× 2
Petunia 'Trailing White'	× 3
Verbena 'Tapien Violet'	× 3

I have chosen a selection of vigorous plants that have quickly filled out this large terracotta urn and tumbled over the edge. If left untamed, they will eventually cover up the pot completely. In this casual style, the plants intermingle, creating a jumbled mass of foliage and flower. There is always a danger that a planting like this will become completely shapeless, with no visual points of reference to hold the eye. The tall column of large Abutilon leaves in the center of the display helps counter this by giving the arrangement some structure and, if the silvery Helichrysum foliage is encouraged to work its way through the trailing white Petunias, it will break up this mass of flowers.

Abutilon 'Nabob' See p.157

Helichrysum petiolare See p.170

PLANTING DETAILS

Planting plan This is an all-around arrangement to be seen from every angle. The Abutilon occupies the center, and the Petunias and Verbenas are spaced equally around the Abutilon, working out toward the rim. The Helichrysums are planted, equally spaced, between the edge of the pot and the center.

Plant care Too much of any one element is not desirable in a mixed planting, so keep watch. Thin out the trailing Petunia occasionally. It is a very vigorous plant and will overwhelm the Verbena and Helichrysum if not kept under control. Also keep the Helichrysum in check to prevent too much foliage from covering the Abutilon.

Helichrysum petiolare 'Limelight' See p.170

CONTAINER DETAILS

Style and **Shape** Though only filled to half its depth to keep the large terracotta urn's weight to a minimum, this container holds plenty of potting mix to support these fast-growing plants. As the plants get bigger, they will need more and more water. Add that to the fact that terracotta is porous and speeds up water evaporation, and you need to take care not to let the potting mix dry out too quickly.

Size Height 32 in (80 cm); Diameter 24 in (60 cm).

Material Terracotta.

Petunia 'Trailing White' See p.179

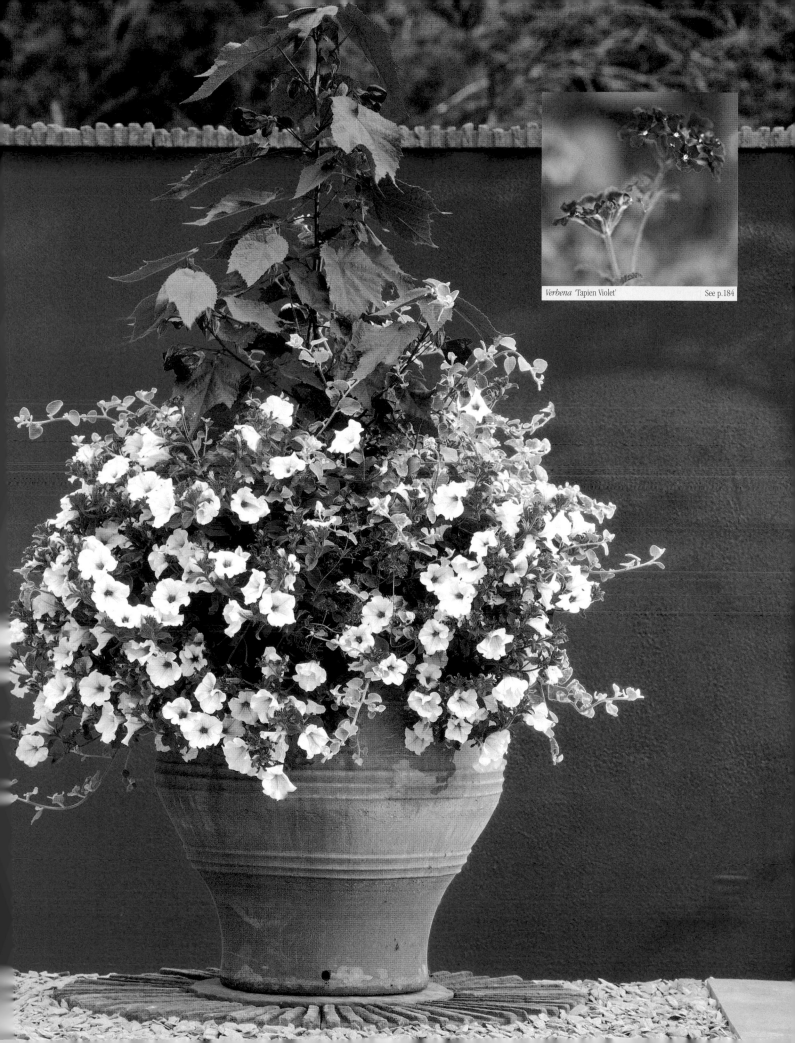

Verbena 'Tapien Violet'   See p.184

Trailing purples

Using flowers within a limited color range ties a theme together, regardless of the choice of plants.

INGREDIENTS	QTY
Salvia splendens 'Purple'	× 5
Verbena 'Diamond Merci'	× 2
Verbena 'Tapien Violet'	× 1
Viola 'Bowles' Black'	× 2

Here, the purple and violet flowering plants have been carefully selected to work well together and to match the gray and blue metallic finish of the planter. To maintain a good sense of proportion, the flowering spires of the Salvias are balanced by the trailing stems of Verbena. The dark metal base of the trough anchors the display and prevents the tall Salvias from making the arrangement appear top-heavy. Within such a planting, I like to add one element, however small, that bends the rules; a small detail that has to be discovered. Here, it is the black Violas, which register as tiny holes of black velvet among the busy foliage.

PLANTING DETAILS

Planting plan This narrow trough has little space from front to back, so the Salvias are packed in as tightly to the back edge as possible. The Verbenas are spaced evenly along the front of the trough, leaving small pockets to tuck in the Violas.

Plant care There is a lot of plant material in a relatively small container, so regular feeding, every two weeks or so, is important to maintain healthy plants. Pinch out the tips of the Verbenas when they are still small to encourage bushy growth, and deadhead the flowers regularly to encourage more to grow.

CONTAINER DETAILS

Style and **Shape** Trough-shaped containers work well in areas of the garden above eye level, such as ledges on the tops of walls or terraces, so the plants can trail down the front edge of the planter. Other site suggestions include using tin trough plantings as window boxes so you can enjoy them from indoors and out. Or make up a series of matching troughs down a set of wide steps to soften harsh lines and allow both flowers and fragrance to spill over from step to step.

Size Height 7 in (18 cm); Width 24 in (60 cm).

Material Galvanized metal.

Salvia splendens 'Purple'   See p.180

Verbena 'Diamond Merci'   See p.185

Verbena 'Tapien Violet'   See p.184

Viola 'Bowles' Black'   See p.185

Fresh lime greens

Simply put, a limited color palette and well-conceived structure equals harmony and balance.

INGREDIENTS	QTY
Adiantum capillus-veneris	× 5
Cordyline australis	× 1
Eucomis bicolor	× 5
Nicotiana 'Lime Green'	× 10

There is great artistic satisfaction to be had from experimenting with plants and pots, and in creating a display that combines shape, color, texture, style, and plant interest by using a very limited yellow-green color palette. This unusual contemporary planting offers a great diversity of plant material, from the spiky leaves of Cordyline through the broad smooth leaves of Eucomis to the soft and feathery fronds of the *Adiantum capillus-veneris* (Maidenhair fern). It carefully brings together a restful color theme with very deliberate contrasts of leaf shape and texture to give it extra appeal.

Adiantum capillus-veneris
See p.157

Cordyline australis
See p. 164

PLANTING DETAILS

Planting plan This display is designed to be viewed from all sides. The key structural plants are the lone Cordyline—plant it first, in the middle. The five Eucomis go in next and are planted toward the rim and spaced evenly around the pot circumference. Plant two Nicotiana between each of the Eucomis. Tuck the ferns around the rim wherever space allows. The Eucomis and Nicotiana are small and then grow to scale, but the Adiantum (Maidenhair fern) and Cordyline need to planted at a mature size because they will only put on a small amount of growth.

Plant care Deadhead the Nicotiana regularly to keep the planting looking its best.

Eucomis bicolor
See p.168

CONTAINER DETAILS

Style and **Shape** This is a large-scale container in a subtle shade of khaki green with a glossy, glazed ceramic finish. The plants have been carefully chosen so they do not detract from its mellow color and simplicity. The container is tall, so to prevent the plant elements from looking squat, I have introduced a Cordyline in the center to add height. On reflection, a slightly taller Cordyline might have been even better.

Size Height 30 in (75 cm); Diameter 24 in (60 cm).

Material Glazed ceramic.

Nicotiana 'Lime Green'
See p.175

Modern rural

*A vivid-colored pot offers an interesting challenge,
which I have met with contrasting and vibrant plants.*

INGREDIENTS	QTY
Hakonechloa macra 'Aureola'	× 4
Petunia 'Million Bells Red'	× 4
Petunia 'Million Bells Cherry'	× 4
Vinca minor 'Illumination'	× 4

Hakonechloa macra 'Aureola'   See p.168

Sometimes the color and surface texture of the container cannot be ignored and should be allowed to lead the planting design. Here, I have selected lime-green and vivid red and deep pink plant colors to draw out the pink and purple tones in the dumpy-shaped glazed ceramic pot. I enjoy using identical plants that have a close but subtly different color relationship. Here I have used two types of Petunia hybrid, one in vivid red and one in deep pink, and set these against variegated lime-green Vinca leaves and Hakonechloa grass. It makes the viewer look twice at the common Petunia and adds an extra dimension that might go unnoticed by some but will raise a wry smile from others.

Petunia 'Million Bells Red'   See p.178

PLANTING DETAILS

Planting plan I used one large Hakonechloa plant that I split into four smaller plants by cutting the roots with a sharp knife and pulling them apart. The Vinca was then planted, evenly spaced, around the edge of the pot. Next, since space in the pot was tight, I arranged the Petunias in among the Vinca and Hakonechloa—anywhere there was room to spare.

Plant care Compared to the more common *Vinca minor*, this variegated type is slow-growing. To encourage faster growth, buy the plants early in the season and give them a head start in a warm, well-ventilated greenhouse.

Petunia 'Million Bells Cherry'   See p.178

CONTAINER DETAILS

Style and **Shape** This low display is small enough to sit on a garden table or plinth outdoors. The flowers and foliage are both small in scale and match the proportions of each other and the ceramic pot. *Petunia* 'Million Bells' is far less vigorous than the more common *Petunia* Surfinia and, to my mind, has greater charm. Its blue-red petals pick up the coloring of the glazed ceramic, while the lime-yellow grass and leaves introduce a citrus note. The pale blue flowers of Vinca that appear late in the season detract from the pink and lime color theme, so I prefer to remove them.

Size Height 14 in (35 cm); Width 16 in (40 cm).

Material Glazed and crazed ceramic.

Vinca minor 'Illumination'   See p.184

Setting standards

Simple shapes, sparse planting, and sympathetic colors give rise to restful and enduring displays.

INGREDIENTS *in each container*	QTY
Bacopa 'White Suttis 98'	× 4
Isotoma (Laurentia) axillaris	× 2
Solanum rantonnetii	× 1

When looking at a group of containers, the eye is usually satisfied by symmetry and balance even if the matches are not exact. Reflected patterns and repeated themes or styles all help to create a reassuring sense of stability. In this display, symmetry is achieved using a standard Solanum plant in each pot with the same quantity of Bacopa and Isotoma plants around the base of each "tree." Both plantings have been installed in similar but not identical pots manufactured from dark gray terrazzo. The slight variation in pot height and shape creates an intriguing imbalance that works to emphasize the symmetry of the plant material rather than disturb it.

Bacopa 'White Suttis 98'   See p.161

PLANTING DETAILS

Planting plan This is an extremely simple planting that achieves its effect from the color and lushness of the Solanums and the fragile look of their slender stems. Each Solanum was planted in the center of its pot and given the extra support of a sturdy garden cane. The Bacopa was arranged around the rim, and the two Isotoma plants were placed in between the Solanum and the Bacopas on the front edge.

Plant care Solanums need regular pinching out to keep their shape and maintain their flowering density. Two full growing seasons would produce standard Solanums of this size. Deadhead the Isotomas to keep them looking neat.

Isotoma (Laurentia) axillaris   See p.172

CONTAINER DETAILS

Style and **Shape** The taller pot is a cylinder and the shorter one a square, but the material is the same. This difference in shape is enough to set each apart but not enough for them to be seen as separate pieces that do not work together as a pair. Gray has a neutral tone that mixes with many colors but seems to work particularly well with blue and purple flower colors.

Size Height 36 in (90 cm); Diameter 16 in (40 cm) *(tall cylinder)*.
Height 24 in (60 cm); Width 16 in (40 cm) *(square container)*.

Material Gray terrazzo.

Solanum rantonnetii   See p.181

Climbers and trailers

A flowery mix in cool colors makes a delightful small planting for the doorstep or patio.

INGREDIENTS	QTY
Antirrhinum 'Trailing White'	× 2
Petunia 'Prism Sunshine'	× 2
Petunia 'White'	× 2
Senecio macroglossus 'Variegatus'	× 3
Thunbergia alata	× 1

In my experience, a lot of flowers can be packed into a small container, and displays grown in these conditions are often subject to the kind of care and attention that simply would not be practical for plants grown in larger gardens. With regular feeding, watering, and deadheading, the display will keep flowering for five months or more. I always try to make the best use of the pot space by growing climbers and trailing plants that thrive in these conditions, such as Thunbergia (black-eyed Susan) and *Senecio macroglossus* 'Variegatus'. I actively encourage the plants to spill out from the pot and go beyond it to create a relaxed, informal arrangement.

Antirrhinum 'Trailing White'
See p.158

Petunia 'Prism Sunshine'
See p.178

PLANTING DETAILS

Planting plan The arrangement was first created without Thunbergia (black-eyed Susan). It was added later when the outdoor temperature had warmed up. A wigwam of sticks was put in at the start. The sticks could have been taller, which would have meant less winding and pinching out of the Thunbergia shoot tips, but it did mean that many shoots wove their way in and through the other plants, putting out bright orange flowers where they were least expected. The Senecio is vigorous and scrambled up the sticks as well as trailing over the rim of the pot. The Antirrhinum flowers come and go in quick bursts of flower throughout the season.

Petunia 'White'
See p.179

CONTAINER DETAILS

Style and **Shape** This dumpy terracotta pot needs both height and trailing stems over its surface to make it appear more elegant. The Thunbergia (black-eyed Susan) gives the display height and the Senecio adds long, trailing stems. As the season progresses, the pot can be raised to allow the Senecio to trail down farther and balance the height of the climbing Thunbergia.
Size Height 11 in (28 cm); Diameter 12 in (30 cm).
Material Machine-made terracotta.

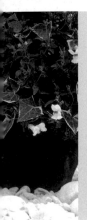

Senecio macroglossus 'Variegatus'
See p.180

Thunbergia alata
See p.183

Desert modern

A pure white trough and succulents that will tolerate hot, dry conditions are ideal for exposed sites.

INGREDIENTS	QTY
Echeveria glauca	× 3
Ophiopogon planiscapus 'Nigrescens'	× 8

This contemporary planting combines nothing more than the well-defined leaf shapes of gray-green Echeveria rosettes with the thin black strands of Ophiopogon grass. Both work together to complement the smooth, clean, rounded shape and white surface of this special trough molded in white composite resin. I enjoy working with a mix of just two plant types; when they are carefully chosen, there is no confusion about the message they send out, and they can make a much bolder statement than more complex arrangements. Also, the simpler the planting plan, the more likely it is that the container will get noticed, and here the great shape, style, and material of this simple trough are shown off to full effect.

PLANTING DETAILS

Planting plan First, the three Echeveria rosettes were planted into the trough. Next, four Ophiopogon grasses were split in half to produce smaller tufts that could be tucked in between and around the rosettes. Any potting mix spilled into the center of the Echeveria was blown out because its abrasive action would have rubbed the beautiful blue-gray bloom off the leaves of these succulents.

Plant care In hard-water areas, try not to spill water on the Echeveria because it will leave behind a noticeable white residue of lime. For the sake of neatness, I like to remove the small lilac flowers of the Ophiopogon, which appear late in the season.

Echeveria glauca See p.167

CONTAINER DETAILS

Style and **Shape** Black and blue-gray foliage make natural color partners, and the contrasting leaf shapes show each other off to best advantage. The long, plain container accentuates the shapely nature of the planting. Nature throws off the color theme by giving the Echeveria pink and yellow flowers—two colors that bear no relation to each other—but I think they add a quirky touch, so I choose to leave them alone in this planting.

Size Height 8 in (18 cm); Length 30 in (75 cm).

Material White composite resin.

Ophiopogon planiscapus 'Nigrescens' See p.174

Pale and hardy

Clean lines, monochrome planting, and simple pot design is a foolproof way to a stylish arrangement.

INGREDIENTS *in rectangular planter*	QTY
Helichrysum italicum	× 3
INGREDIENTS *in tall cylinder*	QTY
Anthemis punctata subsp. *cupaniana*	× 1
Convolvulus cneorum	× 1

This collection of hardy plants favors a sunny position, and the two containers and three plant species have been chosen to create a modern, fairly minimal design. This is achieved by using just two flower colors—white and yellow—and silver foliage. While the foliage in each planting offers variation in leaf shape, the tonal similarity helps keep the whole planting calm. The light pots are plain and regular. The plants are all perennials and evergreen, so with regular feeding and a small amount of deadheading and trimming, these container plantings will provide a long-term display, spanning several growing seasons.

Helichrysum italicum   See p.170

PLANTING DETAILS

Planting plan I planted the Convolvulus toward the back of the circular pot to allow the Anthemis room to spread out and so prevent overcrowding. I then planted three Helichrysums in the trough, following a symmetrical line down the center.
Plant care As the Anthemis matures, flowers will spill down the face of the tall pot. Deadhead the flowers regularly to keep the planting neat and to encourage more flowers after the first early summer flush. Cut back the Helichrysum (curry plant) flowers as soon as they start to lose their color. Make sure that the pots can drain freely, since all these plants need well-drained conditions to stay healthy.

Anthemis punctata subsp. *cupaniana*   See p.158

CONTAINER DETAILS

Style and **Shape** Long, narrow troughs, like long, narrow garden flower borders, create a linear effect because there is no front-to-back dynamic. My advice is to keep the design simple and repeat one theme along its length. Here, I have used three curry scented Helichrysums and added a tall cylinder to break the horizontal, even though I think the trough would hold its own if it stood alone. I have also placed a white stone mulch on the soil surfaces to make the plantings appear even brighter.
Size Height 16 in (40 cm); Width 24 in (60 cm) *(rectangular planter)*.
Height 24 in (60 cm); Diameter 14 in (35 cm) *(tall cylinder)*.
Material White terrazzo.

Convolvulus cneorum   See p.164

Fire-engine red

Red is a passionate color and, love it or hate it, a fire-engine red pot and planting cannot be ignored.

INGREDIENTS	QTY
Pelargonium 'Bushfire'	× 6
Pelargonium 'Ignescens'	× 2
Pelargonium 'Sassy Dark Red'	× 2
Sphaeralcea 'Newleaze Coral'	× 1

When planning a garden border, try limiting yourself to one flower color. This will makes decisions much easier because it drastically reduces the number of plants to choose from.

Exactly the same rules apply—except on a smaller scale—when planting a pot, so if you want to make the design process relatively straightforward, choose plants in just one color. It is made even easier if, as here, you have a fire-engine red pot to show you the way. For maximum impact, I have chosen vivid red petal colors. Subtle tones would also work but lack the immediate impact of these bold hues.

PLANTING DETAILS

Planting plan Pelargoniums provide some of the best and most intense reds and can be guaranteed to put on a good display throughout the summer months if the planter is kept in a sunny position.

Plant care Deadhead the pelargoniums regularly for continuous flowering throughout the summer and to maintain a neat-looking display. Sphaeralcea is a straggly plant and its stems need support. I have pushed some twigs into the soil at the back of the pot and, as the stems develop, I will tie them to the twigs to keep them in check.

Pelargonium 'Bushfire'   See p.176

CONTAINER DETAILS

Style and **Shape** This tall, columnar pot could almost be placed in the garden, unplanted, like a striking piece of modern sculpture. Pots like this are both an inspiration and a challenge. It holds a good quantity of potting mix, though there is no need to fill it completely. To help keep the weight down, use a lightweight filler material (*see page 138*) and then a 16 in (40 cm) depth of potting mix on top.

Size Height 40 in (1 m); Width 14 in (36 cm).

Material Red-sprayed steel.

Pelargonium 'Ignescens'   See p.177

Pelargonium 'Sassy Dark Red'   See p.177

Sphaeralcea 'Newleaze Coral'   See p.183

Purple haze

Two very different plants with similar flowers provide the link that holds this frothy planting together.

INGREDIENTS	QTY
Alyogyne huegelii	× 1
Lotus hirsutus	× 4
Petunia 'Blue Trailing'	× 4
Solenostemon 'Black Prince'	× 4
Viola 'Bowles' Black'	× 4

As many of my container plantings demonstrate, I enjoy large, bold foliage, but I also like to experiment with smaller, less distinct foliage that relies on some characteristic other than its size or architectural shape to create an impression. Here, I have chosen to use *Lotus hirsutus*, which has small, downy gray leaves and a sufficiently tangled way of growing. It looks as if it is bearing the flowers of the Petunia—though, in reality, it has soft, pink-tinged flowers of its own. The Petunia and Alyogyne flowers run from top to bottom of the planting to bring it all together.

Alyogyne huegelii See p.159

Lotus hirsutus See p.173

PLANTING DETAILS

Planting plan The Alyogyne foliage is finely cut and tends to get lost among the Lotus, so a dark barrier of Solenostemon is planted between the two. In displays, I am never sure if I should leave the Solenostemon flowers intact or cut them off. In this case, their light blue color does not cause offense, so they remain. The Alyogyne is planted in the middle of the display with the Solenostemon plants in front and behind. The Lotus are put on either side to increase the width of the planting and so as not to overwhelm the Petunias that are planted in between. The small Violas fit in any leftover space and create dark areas among the foliage.

Petunia 'Blue Trailing' See p.177

CONTAINER DETAILS

Style and **Shape** The container is a very simple, chunky terracotta pot, and when viewed from above, it disappears under a soft, gray frilly skirt and a flourish of blue Petunias. Rightly so. It is the plants and the detail they carry that are important here, not the pot. One concern was that the reddish brown seedpods of the Lotus, which appear in autumn, would conflict with the purple and violet color theme, but this was not the case, and the planting continued to look good until late in the year.
Size Height 15 in (37 cm); Diameter 19 in (48 cm).
Material Terracotta.

Solenostemon 'Black Prince' See p.182

Viola 'Bowles' Black'   See p.185

Quiet sophistication

Green is a calm and soothing color and well-suited to this sophisticated planting for shady spots.

INGREDIENTS	QTY
Asparagus densiflorus	× 1
Aspidistra elatior	× 3
Carex morrowii 'Fisher's Form'	× 2
Tellima grandiflora 'Forest Frost'	× 2

This is a very clever mix of green foliage textures using four well-behaved plants that stay looking remarkably fresh with a minimum of effort. The display uses a diverse mix of foliage to create an arrangement that is both calming because of its color but also visually exciting because of the mixture of shapes. Here, the leaves have been carefully selected so that they range from the very frothy Asparagus fern to the broad and paddlelike Aspidistra, and from the flat and rounded Tellima leaves to the narrow and grasslike strands of Carex.

Asparagus densiflorus   See p.159

Aspidistra elatior   See p.160

PLANTING DETAILS

Planting plan There is a mix of hardy and tender plants being used here. The hardy plants, Tellima and Carex, are evergreen (the Tellima takes on reddish tints in the winter) and can be left in the planter and enjoyed year-round in many areas.

Plant care The Aspidistra and Asparagus need to be lifted out and given indoor protection for the winter. The hole they leave in the planter could be filled with a green form of *Phormium tenax* or a small *Phormium cookianum* 'Tricolor'. Both species would provide good alternative winter interest.

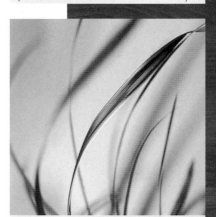

Carex morrowii 'Fisher's Form'   See p.164

CONTAINER DETAILS

Style and **Shape** This Versailles planter has a simple and classic shape that lends itself particularly well to the formal and symmetrical style of this display. Square planters are ideal for arrangements that have a definite front view, and the flat rear side will sit up against the garden wall.

Size Height 18 in (45 cm); Width 18 in (45 cm).

Material Softwood planter, painted dark green.

Tellima grandiflora 'Forest Frost'   See p.182

Exotic explosion

When mixing tender and hardy plants, try to make sure that they have some characteristics in common.

INGREDIENTS	QTY
Cordyline australis 'Torbay Red'	× 1
Helichrysum petiolare 'Limelight'	× 4
Osteospermum jucundum	× 4

In this display, a close visual link is made between the exotic appearance of the hardy *Osteospermum jucundum* and the more tender Cordyline and Helichrysum leaves. The showy flowers of the Osteospermum betray its South African origin and help define its exuberant personality. These flowers sit cheerfully alongside the spiky red Cordyline leaves and the lime-green Helichrysum foliage. As the whole planting matures, the Osteospermum flowers and Helichrysum foliage will spill over the edge of the container. This will make the pot appear less dominant and create a better visual balance, with the tall Cordyline in the center.

Cordyline australis 'Torbay Red'   See p.165

PLANTING DETAILS

Planting plan A square pot is a good shape for a container gardener, since the space available inside makes planting straightforward. Place the Cordyline in the center, one Osteospermum plant in each corner, and each of the four Helichrysums between the Osteospermums along each face of the pot. If the arrangement is only seen from one side, leave out the Helichrysum from the back of the display to allow more space for the roots of the other plants to grow.

Plant care In a sheltered site, both Cordyline and Osteospermum may survive a mild winter. The Helichrysum will not, and is really only a summer addition.

Helichrysum petiolare 'Limelight'   See p.170

CONTAINER DETAILS

Style and **Shape** Cordylines do not increase in size very much during a single season, so choose a plant that balances the scale of the pot. The colors of the Cordyline and Osteospermum have been chosen to complement each other and to contrast in color and texture with the Helichrysum foliage. The silvery gray pot offers a neutral background to lay the flowers and leaves over. Place this planting at the end of a view along a path or through a gateway. Equally, it could take center stage in a small courtyard garden.

Size Height 19 in (48 cm); Width 18 in (45 cm).

Material Glazed frost-resistant ceramic with a gray, semi-matt finish.

Osteospermum jucundum   See p.175

Bright grasses

Strong foliage is the backbone of a successful planting design, in the garden or in a container.

INGREDIENTS *in small container*	QTY
Carex oshimensis 'Evergold'	× 2
Carex phyllocephala 'Sparkler'	× 1
Lamium galeobdolon 'Hermann's Pride'	× 4
INGREDIENTS *in large container*	QTY
Hakonechloa macra	× 3
Liriope muscari 'Variegata'	× 2
Phormium tenax 'Variegatum'	× 1

To my mind, variegated foliage plants are not always very easy to place in the garden; their colored foliage often looks too exotic to fit in easily, while in a container—where we are often expecting the exotic—they look more at home. Strong foliage looks particularly effective when several variegated plants are used in combination, as shown here.

In this grouping, the light green and white color of the foliage has been picked up by the clever choice of pots. The soft yellow flowers of the Lamium are yet to come but will reflect the color of the lime-green ceramic glaze seen on the smaller pot.

Carex oshimensis 'Evergold' See p.163

Carex phyllocephala 'Sparkler' See p.163

PLANTING DETAILS

Planting plan The large pot is planted with the Phormium at the back so that the planting has a front. The smaller pot is planted with its tallest plant in the middle so that it can be viewed from all around.

Plant care This planting uses hardy plants, and *Carex oshimensis* 'Evergold', Liriope, and Phormium are reliably evergreen in warmer regions. Though others are herbaceous, and will die back in winter, a reasonable display can be expected throughout the year with little maintenance. In a very mild winter, *Carex phyllocephala* 'Sparkler' and Lamium will also keep their leaves.

Lamium galeobdolon 'Hermann's Pride' See p.172

CONTAINER DETAILS

Style and **Shape** Using pots in pairs offers extra scope for creating a more interesting display. The pot color can be used to enhance the planting but also to play the pots off against each other. The difference in pot height is another element that the container gardener can exploit. All the variables of tall and short plantings with high and low containers heights should be considered.

Size Height 8 in (20 cm); Width 32 in (80 cm) *(tall pot)*.
Height 15 in (37 cm); Diameter 16 in (40 cm) *(small pot)*.

Material Frostproof glazed ceramic.

Hakonechloa macra   See p.168

Liriope muscari 'Variegata'   See p.173

Phormium tenax 'Variegatum'   See p.178

Abutilon 'Kentish Belle'   See p.157

Sunshine colors

This is a lively, fizzy arrangement where flowers play a major role and foliage provides background "mist."

INGREDIENTS	QTY
Abutilon 'Kentish Belle'	× 1
Antirrhinum Luminaire ™ 'Deep Trailing Yellow'	× 4
Bidens ferufolia 'Golden Star'	× 4
Petunia 'Prism Sunshine'	× 4

The large Petunia flowers and the leaves of the Abutilon are the only elements of any size, and the planting's effectiveness relies on the flowers sitting in a frothy tangle of fine and feathery foliage.

To create the sunny feel, I have used various shades of yellow enriched by the red "cups" (calyces) of the Abutilon, which are also picked up by the reddish buds of the Antirrhinum. The tangle of Bidens and trailing Antirrhinum is self-supporting, but the arching Abutilon stems benefit from some twiggy support to prevent them from falling over as they get longer and heavier with flowers. But leave some Abutilon flowers to flop over into the planting, providing additional color to the body of the display.

Antirrhinum Luminaire ™ 'Deep Trailing Yellow'   See p.158

PLANTING DETAILS

Planting plan In this lively, sun-loving combination, the tall, billowy plants explode from the dark, solid pot like an erupting volcano. The effect is intensified here with sparks of fiery yellow and red that resemble molten lava. The Antirrhinum flowers tend to come in bursts throughout the season, providing a seesaw of anticipation and satisfaction.

Plant care Deadhead the Petunias as they fade to prevent the spent flowers from lying on and rotting the other plants. Some pinching out of the Bidens will be necessary if it is not going to overwhelm everything else.

Bidens ferufolia 'Golden Star'   See p.162

CONTAINER DETAILS

Style and **Shape** The container is a deep steely blue, square metal box—its flat surfaces provide an excellent foil for the flowers and feathery foliage and its solidity makes the planting look even more delicate. Its large size and capacity allow a good front-to-back depth of planting to create rich and abundant arrangements.

Size Height 20 in (50 cm); Width 20 in (50 cm).

Material Lightweight metal with a double skin and a coated surface.

Petunia 'Prism Sunshine'   See p.178

Textured gray-greens

Soft gray-greens and browns are often undervalued, but for subtle, textured displays, they are unbeatable.

INGREDIENTS *in large container*	QTY
Cussonia paniculata	× 1
INGREDIENTS *in small container*	QTY
Dichondra 'Silver Falls'	× 2
Kalanchoe tomentosum	× 1

Cussonia paniculata See p.167

Just three species are on display in this planting, all of them gray, but their differences in leaf shape and habit turn what could be a dismal arrangement into something unique that generates considerable power and dynamism. The textural qualities of the plants begs close-up inspection, not just for visual delight but also for the tactile experience. Dichondra has silky smooth leaves and stems, Kalanchoe has a stiff velvet feel—its brown-edged leaves creating a visual link with the terracotta pots—and the deeply lobed Cussonia foliage is both smooth and leathery.

Dichondra 'Silver Falls' See p.166

PLANTING DETAILS

Planting plan This simple planting requires no specific planting instructions, but the key is to find the right site, free from distracting colors or conflicting textures that are likely to disturb its simplicity.

Plant care To maintain the planting in good health requires little work. The plant that needs most attention is the Dichondra, whose shoots have a tendency to overwhelm the Kalanchoe. To prevent this, trim off shoots as and when required.

Kalanchoe tomentosum See p.173

CONTAINER DETAILS

Style and **Shape** These large and small elliptical terracotta pots are hand-decorated with the same pattern of short gray scratches. They could not be more perfect for this gray themed design. The "teardrop" shape of both pots offers plenty of width for planting but is narrow enough from front to back to stand close to the wall for maximum effect.

Size Height 24 in (60 cm); Width 24 in (60 cm) *(large container)*.
Height 16 in (40 cm); Diameter 14 in (35 cm) *(small container)*.

Material Patterned frostproof terracotta.

Silver selection

A structured jumble of plants can create lots of visual excitement in a pot without appearing chaotic.

INGREDIENTS	QTY
Dichondra 'Silver Falls'	× 3
Elymus magellanicus	× 1
Hebe pimeliodes 'Quicksilver'	× 3
Kleinia senecioides	× 1
Plectranthus argentatus	× 1
Plectranthus cilatus	× 3

This is a glorious mix of textures and shapes within a gray and silver theme. There is not a flower to be seen, but still the eye is led this way and that, skipping from smooth to furry from silky to succulent and from fleshy to filigree. Even when the eye is satisfied, the sense of touch is still in a state of excitement. Run your fingers around the smooth pot for a tactile experience before starting on the numerous plant surfaces. Begin the experience with the pink, velvety stems of *Plectranthus argentatus*.

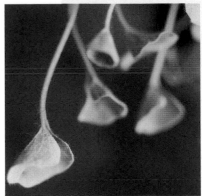

Dichondra 'Silver Falls'   See p.166

Elymus magellanicus   See p.167

PLANTING DETAILS

Planting plan Sadly, the tall center stems of the *Plectranthus argentatus*, which gave the display its height, were damaged and had to be taken out. But their removal exposed the beautiful silvery Elymus grass behind and prevented the Plectranthus from dominating the design. Perhaps, in the future, I will be more deliberately ruthless.

Plant care This planting contains a mix of hardy and tender plants. At the end of the season, remove the hardy Hebe and Elymus. Pot them and leave them outside until next year, or plant them out in the garden until you need them. If you wish to keep the tender plants, pot them and overwinter them in a heated greenhouse.

CONTAINER DETAILS

Style and **Shape** There are so many ingredients in this planting that it is something of a relief that the pot itself has a very smooth surface and a simple, round-bottomed shape; a complete contrast to the frenzied plant-growing activity going on inside.

Size Height 24 in (60 cm); Diameter 16 in (40 cm).

Material Gray composite.

Hebe pimeliodes 'Quicksilver' See p.169

Kleinia senecioides See p.173

Plectranthus argentatus See p.179

Plectranthus cilatus See p.179

Spiky partners

An effective way to show off an enthusiastic collection of succulents is in a bold, simple grouping.

Aeonium arboreum See p.157

INGREDIENTS *in center-front container*	QTY
Aeonium arboreum	× 2
INGREDIENTS *in left container*	QTY
Agave americana 'Variegata'	× 1
INGREDIENTS *in center-back container*	QTY
Aloe ferox	× 1
INGREDIENTS *in right container*	QTY
Opuntia lindheimeri	× 1

Just because you collect plants of a certain genus or type does not mean that you have to treat them like precious gems and hide them away. Almost all species of plants can be shown off in well-chosen, stylish containers that enhance the plants and the collection. Cacti and succulents are particularly good for display because of their architectural shapes. Here, they are planted in a mixed selection of large and small, galvanized and stainless steel planters. Both the durability and the gray color of these metals work well with cacti and succulents, plants that are well-known for their endurance and heat-tolerant nature.

Agave americana 'Variegata' See p.158

PLANTING DETAILS

Planting plan The spiky plants need careful handling. Wear thick leather gloves when planting the Opuntia. To protect your eyes from the sharp leaf tips of the Agave, push corks onto the leaf points or wear goggles as an extra precaution. The Opuntia and Aeonium, in particular, will benefit from being grown in these heavy, and therefore stable, metal pots, particularly as they start to grow bigger and become more and more top-heavy.

Plant care All these plants need good drainage and plenty of sun to thrive.

Aloe ferox See p.159

CONTAINER DETAILS

Style and **Shape** Both galvanized and stainless steel need no maintenance. Brand-new galvanized metal will lose some of its brightness as the surface oxidizes, but stainless steel retains its shiny finish.

Size Height 17 in (42 cm); Width 17 in (42 cm) *(left cube)*.
Height 12 in (30 cm); Length 24 in (60 cm) *(narrow trough)*.
Height 40 in (100 cm); Width 16 in (40 cm) *(center-back cylinder)*.
Height 16 in (40 cm); Width 14 in (36 cm) *(right pot)*.
Material Galvanized metal and stainless steel.

Opuntia lindheimeri See p.174

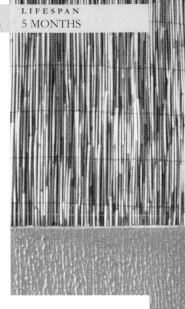

Rambling rhodochiton

Height is often difficult to achieve in containers, but introducing a climber can solve this problem.

INGREDIENTS	QTY
Cerinthe major 'Purpurascens'	× 2
Plectranthus zatarhendii	× 1
Rhodochiton atrosanguineus	× 1

In my experience of tall container designs, it is best to try to achieve a ratio of about one-third pot to two-thirds climber for a balanced look. Climbing plants in pots will need support. For a natural look, I like to use branches cut from trees or shrubs in the garden rather than buying bamboo canes at a garden center. Not only are the curves and bends of the branches more elegant but, on a practical level, the plants cling more readily to their rough surface. Hazel shoots are a good choice because they are both straight and flexible and make ideal supports for climbing plants in pots. Simply push three hazel shoots into a pot, and tie the tips together just below the tops to create a "tepee-style" structure.

Cerinthe major 'Purpurascens'   See p.165

Plectranthus zatarhendii   See p.180

PLANTING DETAILS

Planting plan The three Hazel poles span the soil surface. A single Rhodochiton plant at the foot of one of the poles allows new shoots to climb up all three. The Cerinthe sits in the middle of the pot, using the poles for support as it grows. Like a trailing version of *Plectranthus argentatus*, *P. zatarhendii* spills its velvet-gray foliage over the pot edge. Once it reaches the ground, it is likely to root and provide a quantity of rooted cuttings for other container plantings next year.

Plant care Cerinthe and Rhodochiton produce prolific quantities of seed. Save some at the end of the season to grow next year's plants.

CONTAINER DETAILS

Style and **Shape** This simple planting is inspired by the color and shape of the pot. The glazed pot has a smooth, silky finish: a marvelous foil for the velvet Plectranthus leaves. Its dumpy but upright style is ideal for tall plantings because the relatively broad base helps to stabilize the arrangement, while the eye is carried upward to take in the plants.

Size Height 22 in (55 cm); Diameter 18 in (45 cm).

Material Glazed ceramic.

Rhodochiton atrosanguineus   See p.180

Intensely modern

Plants that are exhibitionists and shout "Look at me!" are often the ones that work well in containers.

INGREDIENTS	QTY
Canna 'Pretoria'	× 3
Cordyline australis Purpurea Group	× 4
Cuphea 'Tiny Mice'	× 3
Uncinia rubra	× 1

This fabulous planting is an excuse to show off the extraordinary leaves and rich orange flowers of *Canna* 'Pretoria' and to create some exotic and colorful excitement just for its own sake. The small Cuphea flowers are such an intense red that they sit like red hot embers in a hearth. They appear to be waiting to be fanned into life in order to set ablaze the grassy leaves of Uncinia and Cordyline, and also to release the flaming orange flowers of the Canna. The tall pot shape helps to raise up the plants to eye level to further increase their dramatic visual impact.

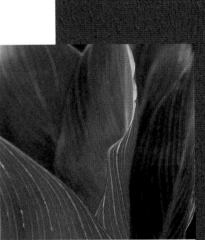
Canna 'Pretoria' See p.162

Cordyline australis Purpurea Group See p.165

PLANTING DETAILS

Planting plan This display shows how simple it is to bring together plants in a range of different sizes in one pot to create a full display. I often use a large Cordyline plant as the central feature in a pot, (*see pages 28-29*) but here I bought some small Cordyline plants that are ideal for tucking in among other busy foliage to add some contrasting spiky structure. Later, the Cordyline will grow into big plants for future use elsewhere, but here they do a perfect job of filling in between the Cannas at the back of the planting and the Cupheas at the front. As a bonus, the color of the Cordyline leaves matches the rust-colored pot surface perfectly.

CONTAINER DETAILS

Style and **Shape** The rust-effect coated steel container has a textured, shiny finish that adds to the sparkle and vigor of the planting. Its height and width are ideal to balance the spread of the wide Canna leaves, which have more growing to do as they exploit the generous amount of potting mix this large container can hold.
Size Height 24 in (60 cm); Width 17 in (42 cm).
Material Rust-effect coated steel.

Cuphea 'Tiny Mice' See p.166

Uncinia rubra See p.184

Regal red and gold

The wind gives life to this planting, as it gently buffets the flowers and swirls the grasses around.

INGREDIENTS	QTY
Carex buchananii	× 1
Osteospermum 'Serena'	× 3
Persicaria microcephala	× 3
Solenostemon hybrid	× 3

Plants are sensitive to changes in light and temperature, and different weather conditions can alter the plant's appearance on a day-to-day or even minute-by-minute basis. This planting was photographed on a sunny but windy day. As the wind picked up, you could catch a glimpse of the wonderful russet colors on the reverse side of petals. On calmer, sunnier days, the apricot-pink Osteospermum flowers are content to open out fully and shine upward from a rich bed of orange and brown foliage, hiding their undersides until the sun goes down and the petals close up, revealing the dark rust beneath.

Carex buchananii   See p.164

Osteospermum 'Serena'   See p.175

PLANTING DETAILS

Planting plan This arrangement is designed to be seen from just one side, even though it is planted in a round container. The grass is planted at the back of the display (rather than in the middle) and every other ingredient is placed in front of the grass to create a forward-facing display.

Plant care This display is a mix of low-maintenance plants that grow up to form a dome-shaped planting. Pinch out the pale blue flowers of Solenostemon (Coleus) so that they do not ruin the fiery red color effect of the foliage. Also, pinch out the growing tips of the Persicaria leaves to control their height and so maintain shape.

Persicaria microcephala   See p.176

CONTAINER DETAILS

Style and **Shape** The half-egg shape of the gray terrazzo pot lends itself to this slightly squat, dome-shaped arrangement, which says, "I am not wild and flamboyant but I am offering you subtle textures and tones of browns and green if you just take the trouble to look."

Size Height 14 in (35 cm); Width 16 in (40 cm).

Material Gray terrazzo.

Solenostemon hybrid   See p.182

Metallic hues

Hardy, year-round plantings can be as exciting and stylish as more exotic summer plantings.

INGREDIENTS *in small container*	QTY
Heuchera 'Silver Scrolls'	× 1
INGREDIENTS *in large container*	QTY
Carex buchananii	× 3
Carex comans 'Frosted Curls'	× 2
Heuchera 'Silver Scrolls'	× 2
Phormium tenax	× 1
INGREDIENTS *in medium container*	QTY
Carex buchananii	× 2
Convolvulus cneorum	× 1
Ophiopogon planiscapus 'Nigrescens'	× 2

Carex buchananii   See p.164

There are very few winter-flowering plants suitable for containers, but that does not mean a winter display has to be dreary. These three pots rely entirely on leaf color and shape for their winter effect. For a seasonal change during the summer months, the Heucheras throw up spikes of flowers, and the Convolvulus sports open white blooms. In a sheltered site, the Heuchera flowers will last into autumn.

Carex comans 'Frosted Curls'   See p.163

PLANTING DETAILS

Planting plan The same principles apply to winter plantings as to summer displays; tall plants at the back with a gradual decrease in scale to the front edge. In the two larger pots, *Phormium tenax* and *Carex buchananii* add height but offer very different styles. Heucheras and Convolvulus fill the foreground. In the largest pot, the long tresses of *Carex comans* 'Frosted Curls' spill down to the ground.

Plant care Plants grow slowly or not at all during the winter, so when planting specifically for winter effect, buy mature plants to get the desired result.

Convolvulus cneorum   See p.164

CONTAINER DETAILS

Style and **Shape** Because of the limited range of plants available for winter displays, the containers themselves play an important part. A matching set of three pots sets the style of the design, and their textured metallic surfaces look great when thrown into relief by the shadows cast by the winter sun.

Size Height 26 in (64 cm); Width 26 in (64 cm) *(large)*.
Height 15 in (38 cm); Width 15 in (38 cm) *(medium)*.
Height 12 in (29 cm); Width 12 in (29 cm) *(small)*.
Material Coated terracotta.

Heuchera 'Silver Scrolls'   See p.171

Ophiopogon planiscapus 'Nigrescens'   See p.174

Phormium tenax   See p.178

Mellow apricots

This warm display blends apricots, oranges, and browns to produce a sumptuous late summer palette.

INGREDIENTS	QTY
Carex flagellifera 'Coca-Cola'	× 3
Lotus maculatus	× 4
Mimulus aurantiacus	× 1
Osteospermum 'Serena'	× 3
Viola 'Apricot'	× 3

This amorphous tangle of flowers and wispy filaments of grass blends together an array of warm, gentle flower and foliage colors to provide an overall mellowness that evokes not autumn but summer evenings when the sun has all but set and its warmth still radiates from the walls and ground. Each flower has a distinct style of its own, and for this reason, no single plant dominates the display. This adds to the relaxed, informal nature of the arrangement, which becomes even more pronounced as the season progresses and the plants start spilling over the edges of the terracotta pot.

Carex flagellifera 'Coca-Cola'   See p.164

Lotus maculatus   See p.174

PLANTING DETAILS

Planting plan *Mimulus aurantiacus* does not know whether it wants to grow upward or sprawl sideways, so I let it do both. I tied some upright shoots to twiggy supports pushed into the middle of the planting and let other shoots spread over the edge of the pot. The Lotus struggled to establish itself and would probably have been better off without so much competition.

Plant care Osteospermums need regular dead-heading to keep the planting neat and, more importantly, to ensure a continuous supply of new flowers.

Mimulus aurantiacus   See p.175

CONTAINER DETAILS

Style and **Shape** There are a lot of plants in this display, and they need plenty of potting mix in order to stay healthy. Fortunately, this wide, almost straight-sided pot has plenty of capacity for potting mix. The rich terracotta color of the pot is ideally suited to the warm colors of the planting.

Size Height 20 in (50 cm); Diameter 24 in (60 cm).

Material Handmade, frostproof terracotta.

Osteospermum 'Serena'   See p.175

Viola 'Apricot'   See p.184

Moody reds

An eruption of sultry red plant material blows out of this large cone with all the drama of a volcano.

INGREDIENTS	QTY
Canna 'Black Knight'	× 3
Dahlia 'Ragged Robin'	× 1
Impatiens 'Accent Cranberry'	× 4
Imperata cylindrica 'Rubra'	× 5

Rich, deep red flower and foliage colors are successfully brought together to create a feeling of fiery sumptuousness and at the same time a moody sense of foreboding. Here, purple-tinged and flame-red foliage are added to a mix of crimson and red flowers to produce a pot full of glowing embers almost waiting to be fanned into flame by the breeze. Using contrasting foliage shapes and textures adds further to the excitement as each vies for attention. The large leaves of the Canna provide a solid background for the frothy Dahlia leaves, while the grassy foliage of Imperata jumps like sparks from the heart of the fire.

Canna 'Black Knight' See p.163

Dahlia 'Ragged Robin' See p.166

PLANTING DETAILS

Planting plan Plant the display from the back to the front of the container. Start with the Cannas, then plant the Dahlias, the Imperatas, and lastly the Impatiens (busy lizzies) in the foreground. At first the design will lack balance as the Dahlia plants grow faster than the Canna, but as the season progresses, it will fill out as planned.

Plant care Use a fertile potting mix and create good drainage to make it possible to grow this mix of plants together (normally they have different cultural requirements). Water and feed the plant material regularly to keep it healthy. Deadhead the Dahlias to encourage the plants to keep flowering.

Impatiens 'Accent Cranberry' See p.170

CONTAINER DETAILS

Style and **Shape** This large galvanized steel cone offers the perfect shape and material for creating a dramatic and moody container display. The conical shape has the effect of thrusting the abundant plant material upward and outward. Combine it with dark, sultry flower and foliage colors and you have a potent and evocative mix.

Size Height 31 in (77 cm); Diameter 24 in (60 cm).

Material Galvanized steel.

Imperata cylindrica 'Rubra' See p.171

Ivy topiary

Tough and reliable container plantings that stay looking good from year to year are to be treasured.

INGREDIENTS *in each container*	QTY
Athyrium filix-femina 'Frizelliae'	× 2
Athyrium niponicum var. *pictum*	× 3
Hedera helix 'Amber Waves'	× 3
Hedera helix 'Lalla Rookh'	× 1

Ivy plants tend to be overlooked by the experienced and amateur gardener alike because they are so common. But with a little imagination, this ubiquitous plant can be grown in pots to create low-maintenance, durable, and stylish displays. Here, to counter the formal style of the topiary ivy "lollipops," each terracotta pot is underplanted with the textured leaves of ferns and a different decorative variety of ivy to add botanical interest as well as a bit of frill. The ferns also provide some seasonal change to the appearance of the display as they die back in winter and then shoot up again in spring.

Athyrium filix-femina 'Frizelliae'   See p.160

Athyrium niponicum var. *pictum*   See p.160

PLANTING DETAILS

Planting plan To create an ivy topiary, take a bushy ivy plant and remove all the trailing stems except for the two longest. Remove all the leaves except the last few at the end of each shoot. Plant it at the base of a strong plastic tube pushed firmly into the potting mix. Wire an upturned hanging basket to the top of the tube. Twist the bare stems in opposite directions around the plastic tube and tie with twine where they cross. Trim out side shoots as the main shoots grow upward. When the shoots reach the basket, weave them through the holes to form a full head of ivy.

Plant care Trim off any wayward shoots to keep the ball-shaped heads compact.

Hedera helix 'Amber Waves'   See p.169

CONTAINER DETAILS

Style and **Shape** I have chosen simple terracotta pots to counteract the busy planting. Because it is a permanent display, I have used straight-sided pots that hold as much potting mix as possible. Also, the wide pot bases help to prevent these top-heavy trees from blowing over in high winds.

Size Height 10 in (26 cm); Width 20 in (50 cm) *(two identical containers)*.

Material Terracotta.

Hedera helix 'Lalla Rookh'   See p.169

Solid structures

Carefully chosen plants and distinctive containers combine to create a warm but modern look.

INGREDIENTS *in small planter*	QTY
Askiodiosperma paniculatum	× 1
INGREDIENTS *in medium planter*	QTY
Calopsis paniculata	× 2
INGREDIENTS *in large planter*	QTY
Chondropetalum mucronatum	× 2

Containers made from wood have a natural affinity with plants. They will survive quite happily outdoors, and many wooden planters actually improve with age as their surface becomes weathered. Wooden planters are often associated with traditional or country garden styles, but solid wood planters in simple designs can produce plantings for the most contemporary garden setting. Here, I have chosen simple wood container shapes and used only a limited range of evergreen plants, selected because they belong to the same family. It is an understated and restful plant combination—all the more restful because it requires little aftercare.

Askiodiosperma paniculatum   See p.159

Calopsis paniculata   See p.163

PLANTING DETAILS

Planting plan All three plants belong to the family Restionaceae, members of which are usually known as Restios. They grow best in acidic soil. To make life easier, plant just one species per container so that you do not have to worry about satisfying the needs of several different types of plant in one place. A group of three planters also gives you the opportunity to arrange each one so that it looks its best. I chose these Restios for their obvious architectural strengths, their evergreen nature, and the brownish color of their bracts, which ties the planting to the color of the wood.
Plant care Water the plants with soft water to maintain soil acidity.

CONTAINER DETAILS

Style and **Shape** These "Versailles-gone-modern" planters offer the enduring appeal of traditional wooden tubs, but with a sharper, modern edge. They come with a metal liner to help protect the wooden outer casing from soil moisture but also to make it easier to repot or transplant whatever is growing inside.
Size Height 17 in (43 cm); Width 17 in (43 cm) *(small planter)*.
Height 21 in (52 cm); Width 21 in (52 cm) *(medium planter)*.
Height 28 in (71 cm); Width 28 in (71 cm) *(large planter)*.
Material Solid oak.

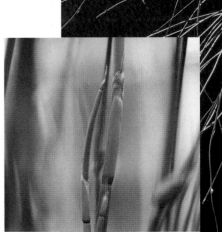

Chondropetalum mucronatum   See p.164

Shades of purple

Begonias are well-known as houseplants but will enjoy a summer holiday outdoors in containers.

INGREDIENTS *in container on ground*	QTY
Begonia 'Connie Boswell'	× 1
Begonia 'Fireworks'	× 1
Begonia 'Solid Silver'	× 1
Tradescantia pallida 'Purpurea'	× 1
INGREDIENTS *in trough on wall*	QTY
Begonia 'Martin Johnson'	× 1
Begonia 'Peace'	× 2
Ipomoea batatas 'Blackie'	× 1

In my experience, popular houseplants like Tradescantia, Chlorophytum (Spider plant), Solenostemon (Coleus), and Begonias, which are used to languishing indoors on a windowsill for most of the year, get a new lease on life when given the opportunity to grow outdoors during the summer months. Here, Tradescantia and a selection of ornamental Begonias form the foundation of this trough and tub display. The plants grow so well outdoors when given a good depth of soil and favorable growing conditions that they become almost unrecognizable as the indoor specimens.

Begonia 'Connie Boswell'　　　See p.161

Begonia 'Fireworks'　　　See p.160

PLANTING DETAILS

Plant care Usually, I grow all the plants in my container displays in a loam-based potting mix, but for Begonias I use a peat-based mix, which they prefer. These very ornamental Begonias can take a surprising amount of direct sunlight, but too much heat can make the leaves lose their distinctive coloring and lustrous leaf gloss. Begonias are best grown in a well-lit position but out of direct sunlight. These conditions will also suit the other plants in the display. If well fed and watered, Begonia varieties like 'Peace' and 'Solid Silver' will produce spectacularly big leaves.

Begonia 'Solid Silver'　　　See p.161

CONTAINER DETAILS

Style and **Shape** I have used two different metal containers to complement the metallic sheen of the Begonia leaves. The trough has a smooth galvanized steel finish, while the tub is an old copper cistern rescued from a junkyard. They make a good pair but will also work equally well on their own.
Size Height 8 in (20 cm); Width 32 in (80 cm) *(trough)*.
Height 15 in (37 cm); Diameter 16 in (40 cm) *(pot on ground)*.
Material Galvanized steel trough and reclaimed copper tub.

Tradescantia pallida 'Purpurea'　　　See p.184

Begonia 'Martin Johnson'   See p.161

Begonia 'Peace'   See p.161

Ipomoea batatas 'Blackie'   See p.171

Low-maintenance pink

Although this mauve-pink Osteospermum looks rather exotic, it is in fact a hardy plant.

Heuchera 'Plum Pudding'　　　　See p.171

INGREDIENTS	QTY
Heuchera 'Plum Pudding'	× 1
Osteospermum jucundum	× 4

The hardy nature and evergreen foliage of *Osteospermum jucundum* are very useful assets to the gardener. Its beauty lies in the fact that it can be set up in a container and left outside all year round in milder areas. When the warmer weather comes, the Osteospermum produces long-stemmed, daisylike flowers that will bloom from late spring to autumn. The Heuchera is equally low-maintenance, with its foliage providing year-round interest and then, in summer, throwing up tall spikes of tiny flowers. A row of pots along a path edge or sunny wall using this Osteospermum and Heuchera mix will provide good year-round interest with the minimum of cost or maintenance—very effective and very simple.

Osteospermum jucundum　　　　See p.175

PLANTING DETAILS

Planting plan This is simplicity itself. Plant the Heuchera in the center of the pot and equally space the four Osteospermums around it. Once established, the Osteospermums will spread out quickly to fill the spaces in between.

Plant care Here are two self-sufficient plants that need little care. Plant both the Osteospermum and Heuchera in a loam-based potting mix and make sure they are fed regularly throughout the growing season. Shelter the pot from cold winds so that the Heuchera foliage does not become wind-scorched.

CONTAINER DETAILS

Style and **Shape** Long-term plantings need a large volume of potting mix to stay healthy. Straight-sided pots hold the maximum amount of soil for a given diameter, but this slightly flared pot offers both a visually pleasing shape and a generous interior space for plant growth. The container's silky black finish complements the dark plum Heuchera leaves.

Size Height 16 in (40 cm); Diameter 18 in (45 cm).

Material Black glazed ceramic.

Textured trail

Low, wide containers are a useful addition to the courtyard garden, and they look great in paved areas.

INGREDIENTS	QTY
Asparagus densiflorus	× 4
Pelargonium 'Lady Plymouth'	× 4
Plectranthus madagascariensis Variegated mintleaf	× 4
Senecio petasitis	× 1

Low plantings sit on the ground—well below eye level—which makes them ideal for placing in front of garden ornaments, like statuary, since they will not interrupt your line of vision. Low container plantings can also work well when placed near a favorite garden bench or in front of a group of taller containers, where they will have the effect of spreading and enriching all the other container-grown material. In most cases, the style of the pot is not really important because it will not be seen. The low arrangement will be looked down on, and a full and healthy planting will have filled out and trailed over the edges of the container well before the end of the season.

Asparagus densiflorus   See p.159

PLANTING DETAILS

Planting plan The pot is planted in a classic configuration, with the tall Senecio planted in the center of the display and three concentric circles of different foliage plants around it. This arrangement relies on the fresh green tones of variegated leaves and will thrive in light shade.

Plant care As the season progresses, the Senecio will get taller, but if you pinch out the growing tips early on, it will fill out and become bushier. Encourage the Plectranthus to trail across the paving with the occasional strand running back into and through the feathery Asparagus fronds and the large Senecio leaves.

CONTAINER DETAILS

Style and **Shape** The main drawback of using a shallow container is that it holds a smaller volume of potting mix than a deeper pot. This may limit the plants' potential growth. When choosing a low container, try to find one that has a wide diameter—as seen here—to compensate for the shallow depth.

Size Height 12 in (30 cm); Diameter 28 in (70 cm).

Material Terracotta.

Pelargonium 'Lady Plymouth'   See p.177

Plectranthus madagascariensis   See p.179

Senecio petasitis   See p.181

Flame colors

Orange is a color avoided by many gardeners, but for what reasons, it is hard to understand.

INGREDIENTS	QTY
Begonia fuchsioides	× 4
Canna musifolia	× 2
Canna Orange hybrid	× 2
Crocosmia 'Star of the East'	× 2
Isoplexis canariensis	× 1
Pelargonium tomentosum	× 1

I find that the trick with using orange flowers successfully in plantings is to mix them in with plenty of greenery so that they do not overpower the arrangement. I also try to mix up pure orange flowers with other shades of orange and closely associated vibrant reds. This jam-packed collection of lush foliage produces a well-balanced effect. Here, the green foliage is more dominant and the orange flowers peer out from between the leaves, but without their fire, I think the arrangement would fall flat.

Begonia fuchsioides — See p.162

Canna musifolia — See p.162

PLANTING DETAILS

Planting plan *Canna musifolia* is planted across the back edge of this square pot. I split a large clump into several small pieces and strung them out in a line so that their huge leaves provide a solid backdrop to the planting. The Isoplexis is planted in the pot center for height and is grown as a standard on a clear stem. The *Begonia fuchsioides* are planted around the base of the Isoplexis on each side, with the short Canna hybrids planted at the front edge. The soft-leaved Pelargonium then sits between these Canna hybrids.

Plant care This lush planting needs plenty of water and weekly feeding to sustain it.

Canna Orange Hybrid — See p.162

CONTAINER DETAILS

Style and **Shape** This is the kind of container shape that I enjoy. Its scale is big, so I can use large plants and get plenty of front-to-back depth in the planting. It has a great volume, which I can fill with plenty of potting mix to support the amount of growth I expect. Lastly, the container surface carries the minimum of decoration, so it does not detract from the beauty of the plants.

Size Height 24 in (60 cm); Width 26 in (65 cm).

Material Plastic faux terracotta.

Crocosmia 'Star of the East' — See p.165

Isoplexis canariensis   See p.171

Pelargonium tomentosum   See p.176

Shade-loving foliage

Strong foliage shapes in fresh minty greens and whites add a bright note to a shady corner of the garden.

Aegopodium podagraria 'Variegatum' See p.157

INGREDIENTS *in left container*	QTY
Aegopodium podagraria 'Variegatum'	× 1
INGREDIENTS *in center-back container*	QTY
Petasitis japonicus 'Nishiki-buki'	× 1
INGREDIENTS *in right container*	QTY
Tolmiea menziesii 'Taff's Gold'	× 3

There are certain plants that have an invasive nature, and no matter how attractive they look, you need to be very wary of letting them loose in your garden. Growing them in the confines of a pot is the ideal solution, since it enables you to enjoy them without fear that they will overwhelm your other garden plants. In this arrangement, both Aegopodium and Petasites are invasive, but they have very good-looking foliage that is fabulous when grown in containers alongside Tolmiea. All three plants will do well in a shady part of the garden where flowery plants would struggle to perform.

PLANTING DETAILS

Planting plan With just one plant species in each pot, planting is extremely easy. To cover the pot more quickly, split the single Aegopodium plant into several smaller parts. All three are hungry plants, so add some controlled-release fertilizer to each of their potting mixes before planting.

Plant care These hardy perennials can be left in their pots all year, although they will die back in winter. They will benefit from regular feeding and should be repotted after two or three years—be careful where you discard any unwanted pieces of Petasites plant material, since they are likely to root themselves and spread.

CONTAINER DETAILS

Style and **Shape** This is a low planting, and when viewed from above, the pots are barely visible. I have used three plain, black glazed pots. They are slightly different in shape and size to give some interest when the plants die back in the winter.

Size Height 9 in (23 cm); Diameter 15 in (37 cm) *(left)*.

Height 14 in (34 cm); Diameter 16 in (38 cm) *(center)*.

Height 16 in (38 cm); Width 13 in (33 cm) *(right)*.

Material Glazed ceramic.

Petasitis japonicus 'Nishiki-buki' See p.177

Tolmiea menziesii 'Taff's Gold' See p.183

Bright and bold

Don't shy away from brightly colored containers; use them to inspire bold and modern plantings.

INGREDIENTS	QTY
Geranium 'Ann Folkard'	× 2
Penstemon 'Blackbird'	× 1
Salvia farinacea 'Victoria'	× 4
Tibouchina urvilleana	× 1

This vivid blue metal container has an intensity of color that is difficult to match in nature. However, I decided to rise to the challenge and find vivid-colored flowers that would hold their own when forming an alliance with this intense blue partner. Tibouchina, Geranium, and Penstemon in shades of purple and magenta work well because they have enough blue in their color makeup to link them to the pot, as well as red tones to help them stand out. Purple Salvias are also good allies because their flowers contain a mixture of blue and red hues.

Geranium 'Ann Folkard'   See p.169

Penstemon 'Blackbird'   See p.176

PLANTING DETAILS

Planting plan Tibouchina is central to this arrangement and usually produces a mass of large, very showy purple flowers, but my two plants refused to flower. *Salvia farinacea*, planted in front of the Tibouchina, performed well, as did the lime-green-leaved *Geranium* 'Anne Folkard', planted along the front edge of this square pot. Later in the season, the old leaves of Tibouchina turn bright orange before they drop off. If you do not wish to upset the carefully controlled balance, you may find these leaves disturbing; here, I saw it as an advantage because it helped to spice up the display.

Plant care Train the vigorous Geranium shoots away from the center of the planting.

Salvia farinacea 'Victoria'   See p.181

CONTAINER DETAILS

Style and **Shape** The bowed sides of this square container give it a slightly dumpy appearance. To slim down the pot shape, it helps to grow trailing plants over the sides. I have used the hardy *Geranium* 'Anne Folkard', but it is very vigorous and will need to be thinned out as the season progresses if the pot is to remain visible.

Size Height 24 in (60 cm); Width 18 in (44 cm).

Material Powder-coated steel.

Tibouchina urvilleana   See p.183

Luscious leaves

*Matching a pot to a plant is container gardening
at its simplest but, potentially, most powerful.*

INGREDIENT *in left container*	QTY
Begonia 'Comtesse de Montesquieu'	× 3
INGREDIENT *in center container*	QTY
Solenostemon 'Juliet Quartermain'	× 1
INGREDIENT *in right container*	QTY
Begonia 'Fire Flush'	× 3

A group of three separate containers, each planted with a different but well-chosen leafy plant, can offer an attractive alternative to a mixed planting. Each separate element also has flexibility because it can be moved around or repositioned against a suitable background color or texture to reinforce the overall design. This style of display will also satisfy the avid plant collector who wants to be able to enjoy the distinctive character of the plant's attributes in isolation, without compromising the group dynamic; for a gardener, to grow plants in this controlled way surely offers the best of both worlds.

Begonia 'Comtesse de Montesquieu'See p.160

PLANTING DETAILS

Plant care Growing just one species per pot means that you do not have to concern yourself with plant compatibility or creating the best conditions to make every species happy. You can simply provide the one plant with the conditions it needs to grow well. In this grouping, I found that the two pots that hold the Begonias have rims that turn inward, making it difficult to lift out the established Begonia plants to repot them. To make the Begonia plants easier to move when mature, first plant them into a smaller plastic pot, to contain their roots, and then place the plastic pot inside the ceramic one.

CONTAINER DETAILS

Style and **Shape** This arrangement uses a subtle rust color palette, but for added interest the pots are slightly different in color and have very different finishes. The two Begonia pots have a stony, matt surface and the tall cylinder, a glossy ceramic glaze—a difference not big enough to upset the planting but enough to make you look again.
Size Height 14 in (36 cm); Width 14 in (36 cm) *(left and right)*.
Height 17 in (42 cm); Diameter 14 in (36 cm) *(center)*.
Material Stone composite (left and right) and glazed ceramic (center).

Solenostemon 'Juliet Quartermain'   See p.183

Begonia 'Fire Flush'   See p.160

Rusty hues

I like to liven up permanent plantings by throwing one or two colorful plants into the mix in summer.

INGREDIENTS	QTY
Carex flagellifera 'Coca-Cola'	× 4
Crocosmia 'Star of the East'	× 3
Cuphea ignea	× 1
Thunbergia alata	× 1

My garden flower borders benefit from the addition of tender plants in the warm summer months, and I like to treat my permanent container plantings in the same way, choosing colors and styles of flowers that will enhance the more established residents. First, the display has to be neatened up to make room for some fresh potting mix and the tender Cuphea and Thunbergia plants. This means cutting back the wispy Carex grass and cutting out some of the deep Crocosmia roots. Fortunately, most plants are able to withstand a certain amount of root damage, especially when they are actively growing. I find that the serrated blade of a bread knife is the ideal tool for cutting out these tough roots.

Carex flagellifera 'Coca-Cola'   See p.164

Crocosmia 'Star of the East'   See p.165

PLANTING DETAILS

Planting plan This simple-looking planting needs a certain amount of preplanning. The hardy Carex grasses form the backbone of the planting and are beautiful in their own right, but to add some late-season color, Crocosmia corms were planted into the pot the previous autumn. Their flowers range in color from soft yellow to intense red and they make very good hardy container plants. Prior to flowering, Crocosmias will also provide good green foliage. Thunbergia and Cuphea are tender and are should be planted in late spring when the weather improves and the danger of frost has passed.

Cuphea ignea   See p.166

CONTAINER DETAILS

Style and **Shape** This square, reeded pot was chosen so that its straight lines and formal look would set off the informal, fluffy character of the Carex grass. The pot also contributes a certain amount of style and interest during the winter months when only the grass is showing. Also, its pinkish terracotta coloring is well suited to the earthy brown and orange tones that characterize this display.
Size Height 20 in (50 cm); Width 16 in (40 cm).
Material Plastic faux terracotta.

Thunbergia alata   See p.183

Bluegrass melody

Large-scale plantings in huge pots are as impressive as garden sculpture—go big, bold, and dramatic.

INGREDIENTS	QTY
Argyranthemum foeniculaceum	× 4
Ceropegia linearis subsp. *woodii*	× 6
Leymus arenarius	× 3
Helichrysum petiolare	× 4
Melianthus major	× 1

There is plenty of room in this large but lightweight square metal container, which provides an exciting opportunity to create a dramatic large-scale arrangement. The scale and size of the container actually demand an extravagant planting style with a head-turning selection of leaf shapes and textures. Also, the sheer volume of potting mix that it can hold means that all five plants will have enough space and nutrients to achieve healthy and vigorous growth. The flamboyant display will suit a range of garden locations, but wherever it is placed, it is asking to be the center of attention and should be given a prominent position where it can stand alone.

Argyranthemum foeniculaceum   See p.159

Ceropegia linearis subsp. *woodii*   See p.165

PLANTING DETAILS

Planting plan The huge metal pot and the large gray-leaved Melianthus were the inspiration for the whole planting, which follows a gray/white color theme. The dramatic planting includes the vigorous blue-gray grass *Leymus arenarius*. This is an invasive plant but safe when grown in the confines of a pot. *Helichrysum petiolare*— another vigorous plant—was also chosen for its silvery leaves, Argyranthemum to add some highlights of white, and Ceropegia to contribute some interesting leaf detail and to help cover the sides of the pot. All the foliage was planted from the center out, and evenly spaced around the Melianthus plant in the middle of the pot.

Helichrysum petiolare   See p.170

CONTAINER DETAILS

Style and **Shape** At 36 in (90 cm) high and 24 in (60 cm) square, the container is big and looks big, so it is important to use plants like Ceropegia that trail over the sides and visually reduce the container's bulk. Despite its solid appearance, the planter is made from a double skin of thin metal, so it is lighter than it looks. When planted, it is only half-filled with potting mix to help keep down its overall weight.
Size Height 36 in (90 cm); Width 24 in (60 cm).
Material Twin-walled, zinc-coated metal.

Leymus arenarius   See p.173

Melianthus major   See p.174

Contemporary display

Take note: flowers can be temperamental and may not always perform, but good foliage is always reliable.

INGREDIENTS	QTY
Carex flagellifera 'Coca-Cola'	× 3
Dahlia 'Bednall Beauty'	× 3
Kleinia senecioides	× 1
Salvia 'Raspberry Royale'	× 2

I chose this variety of Dahlia because of its ability to produce an abundant display of very deep red flowers over a sustained period and because it has beautiful dark feathery foliage.

Carex flagellifera 'Coca-Cola'   See p.164

However, when I planted the trough, the Dahlias produced flower buds that refused to open. The idea behind this planting was to produce an arrangement that provides layers of contrast of texture and shape. In theory, the Dahlia and Salvia flowers appear together with a similar color and intensity and tie the planting together. The succulent, *Kleinia senecioides* (Senecio) is added for its texture and to break up the mass of the dark Dahlia foliage and soften the front edge of the container.

PLANTING DETAILS

Plant care To encourage the Dahlias to spill forward over the edge of the metallic trough, I pinched out the tips to a forward-facing bud when the plants were young. As these shoots become heavier and grow toward the light, they naturally lean forward. Later in the season, the Carex puts out grassy flowers on long stalks, adding a more graceful and softer look to the display. The foliage of *Kleinia senecioides* (Senecio) will also spill over and reach the ground well before the end of the season. Deadheading the Dahlia flowers is also important for maintaining a succession of flowers.

CONTAINER DETAILS

Style and **Shape** Troughs of this size and capacity are ideal for creating full, dense plantings. They work well when arranged in groups in contemporary courtyard areas where a square or geometric look is all-important. Troughs provide a good length of display without projecting too far forward, making them the perfect shape for a narrow walkway or anywhere space is limited.
Size Height 16 in (40 cm); Width 34 in (85 cm).
Material Powder-coated steel.

Dahlia 'Bednall Beauty'   See p.167

Kleinia senecioides   See p.173

Salvia 'Raspberry Royale'   See p.181

Lemon layer cake

I think of this display as an "aromatic layer cake" to be enjoyed in a shady corner of a warm garden.

Alocasia sanderiana See p.159

INGREDIENTS	QTY
Alocasia sanderiana	× 5
Fatsia japonica	× 1
Pelargonium 'Lady Plymouth'	× 5

Aromatic citrus scents are usually associated with the sun-loving foliage of Mediterranean shrubs, but here I have chosen the delicious eucalyptus and lemon fragrance of *Pelargonium* 'Lady Plymouth', which favors half-shade. This Pelargonium not only smells wonderful but produces attractive variegated green leaves. Sitting above the Pelargoniums are the large white-veined leaves of Alocasia. They need plenty of warmth to reach their full size, but the shapes of the smaller leaves still offer a welcome contrast to the glistening Fatsia foliage above and the variegated Pelargonium leaves below.

PLANTING DETAILS

Planting plan This domed display is designed to be seen from all sides and is very simple to plant. The Fatsia sits in the center, the Pelargoniums are evenly spaced around the rim, and the Alocasias fill in the gaps between.

Plant care Take care not to let the Pelargonium foliage overwhelm the Alocasia. The flowers on *P.* 'Lady Plymouth' are small and pink. In my opinion, they ruin the leafy green effect and should be pinched off periodically.

CONTAINER DETAILS

Style and **Shape** Here is a gloriously rotund, white crackle-glazed pot with enough of a hint of blue to cool the white almost to ice. Too cold, I thought at first, but as the Alocasia leaves developed, they carried the blue tones into the planting, lessening the cold effect. Ceramic pots of these dimensions are heavy and, once planted, are difficult to move. Choose a place for the pot and position it before planting.

Size Height 20 in (50 cm); Width 24 in (60 cm).

Material White glazed ceramic.

Fatsia japonica   See p.169

Pelargonium 'Lady Plymouth'   See p.177

container
materials

Container choice

Available in a host of new and traditional materials,
the choice of outdoor containers has never been better.

The upsurge in small-space living and a desire for instant results has renewed people's interest in container gardening. This, in turn, has led to huge innovations in pot design and use of materials from which they are made. Traditional container materials like terracotta and stone are being used to create modern adventurous designs, while experiments with new materials like molded resin have given rise to an unprecedented choice of planters. There is now a style, shape, size, and color of pot for every gardening situation, and if what you want doesn't exist, a custom planter or group of planters can be commissioned at a reasonable rate. Such variety of containers gives ample scope for innovation and indulgence.

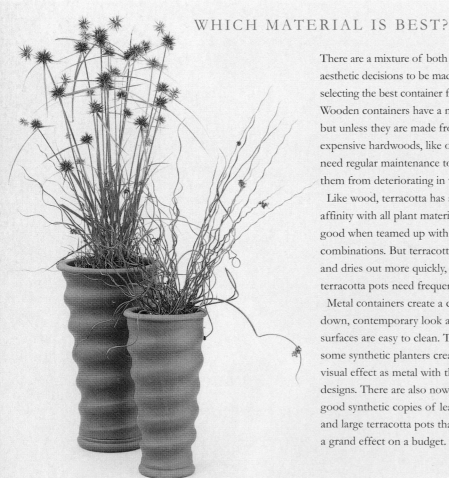

WHICH MATERIAL IS BEST?

There are a mixture of both practical and aesthetic decisions to be made when selecting the best container for your needs. Wooden containers have a natural appeal, but unless they are made from the more expensive hardwoods, like oak, they will need regular maintenance to prevent them from deteriorating in wet weather.

Like wood, terracotta has a natural affinity with all plant material and looks good when teamed up with most plant combinations. But terracotta is porous and dries out more quickly, so plants in terracotta pots need frequent watering.

Metal containers create a clean, pared-down, contemporary look and their hard surfaces are easy to clean. Terrazzo and some synthetic planters create the same visual effect as metal with their simple designs. There are also now some very good synthetic copies of lead cisterns and large terracotta pots that can create a grand effect on a budget.

Clay

A common and versatile material suitable for a variety of garden styles. It is available as traditional terracotta or with a glaze applied to the surface in a wide range of colors and finishes.

- Unglazed terracotta is porous and therefore plant-friendly. It carries air to the plant roots.
- Unglazed terracotta takes latex, paint giving you an unlimited color range.
- Clay pots are heavy and so bring stability to large or top-heavy plantings.

- Unglazed terracotta absorbs water from the potting mix, so the plants need to be watered more frequently.
- If water seeps in beneath the glaze, the pot is prone to frost damage.
- Clay pots are likely to break if they are dropped or accidentally tip over.

Wood

The only container material that is a renewable resource. Natural wood planters, available in soft- and hardwoods, are unobtrusive and blend well with plant material.

- Wood is easy to work and light to handle, making it ideal for producing your own plant containers at home.
- It is impervious to frost.
- Wood takes paints and stains, so colors can be changed or refreshed each year.

- Wood planks can only be made into square or rectangular shapes, so only a few designs are possible.
- Life is short if the wood is untreated.
- Painted softwood needs regular maintenance to prevent it from rotting.

Stone

Though often regarded as a traditional material for classic-style urns, modern techniques have produced a host of exciting stone containers in contemporary shapes and styles.

- Nonporous, so does not dry out the potting mix too quickly.
- Strong and durable.
- Stone compounds are readily molded, so there is a broad range of shapes, and patterns from complex to plain and simple are available.

- All stone products are heavy, which makes them very stable but often extremely difficult to move to another location without help.
- Stone containers can be expensive.

Metal

Originally, metal containers were recycled utilitarian items like animal troughs and water cisterns. However, new ways of working with metal have led to more adventurous pot designs.

- Good choice of shapes, colors, and finishes in old, recycled, and new pots.
- Stylish designs available. Metal finishes are ideal for clean contemporary design.
- Frostproof.

- Steel containers are prone to rust, so choose products with quality coatings if you want your containers to last.
- May scratch or dent.
- Poorly galvanized products can have dangerously sharp or rough edges.

Synthetic

Made from plastics, polymers, fiberglass, and resins, synthetic containers are available in almost any color, shape, texture or finish.

- Synthetic materials are usually tough but lightweight, making them suitable for roof terraces and balconies.
- Frostproof.
- Faux stone, metal, and terracotta pots in traditional designs are available at a fraction of the cost of the real thing.

- Abrasions and scuffs can cause permanent damage.
- Poor copies can look cheap and artificial.
- The pot surface does not age well or develop an attractive patina like containers made of natural materials.

Clay

This natural material can be hand-thrown on a potter's wheel, shaped in a mold, or built up in coils.

The beauty of natural clay is that its color can vary from pale pink to deep rich reds and grays, depending on the source of the clay. The best terracotta pots are handmade, and the only ones I avoid are those that have a very narrow neck because they can break in cold weather when the potting mix inside freezes and then expands as it thaws. Before the pots are fired in the kiln, the clay surface can be easily scored, pressed, and patterned to provide a range of textures and finishes. They can be elaborately decorated with molded swags and nymphs, or more simply decorated with latticework or a repeat pattern.

If you like this traditional material but want something that looks modern, buy clay pots that have been glazed in contemporary colors. In my view, single-color glazes are inspirational, while mixed-color glazes can be distracting and difficult to use in combination with plant material.

Terracotta is the ideal material for country-style plantings like this. Within two or three seasons, this pale-surfaced pot will age beautifully, building up a rich patina of color as a result of algal growth. The algae live on the crusted salts and nutrients that leach out through the porous terracotta surface from the potting mix when the planting is watered.

SOAKING TERRACOTTA BEFORE PLANTING

Terracotta pots are ideal containers for plants because they are porous and allow air to reach the roots, but the natural porosity of this material also creates problems, especially for young plants. Dry terracotta pots will soak up any excess water from the potting mix and dry it out completely, depriving young plants of much-needed moisture. To help prevent the plants from drying out, give them an extra-thorough watering before planting, and also soak your empty terracotta in a bucket of water so that it is fully saturated with liquid.

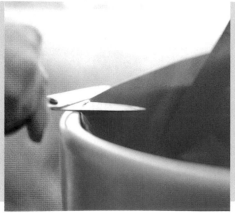

LINING GLAZED POTS WITH PLASTIC

Glazed clay pots that have not been glazed on the inner surface and those with a crackle glaze finish are vulnerable to frost damage (*see page 148*) because water can seep in under the glaze. To prevent frost damage, line the insides with a layer of heavy-duty plastic sheeting to make them waterproof. Here, I have used blue plastic, but clear, black, or green may be more suitable in a garden setting. Make sure the lining has a generous overlap and extends all the way down to the base of the pot without covering the drainage hole. This waterproof lining technique will also prevent salts from leaching through a crackle glaze finish and will ensure that the outer surface of the pot stays clean.

A selection of clay containers

Sizes are shown as *height x diameter*

1 Lime glazed clay pot; *15in (37cm) x 16in (40cm)*
2 Hand-thrown terracotta spiral; *14in (35cm) x 8in (20cm)*
3 Metallic painted terracotta; *12in (29cm) x 12in (29cm)*
4 Flame red glazed ceramic; *15in (37cm) x 16in (40cm)*
5 Hand-finished terracotta; *4in (10cm) x 8in (20cm)*
6 Hand-thrown terracotta pot; *21in (53cm) x 18in (45cm)*
7 Hand-decorated terracotta; *16in (40cm) x 14in (35cm)*
8 Hand-decorated terracotta; *6in (15cm) x 12in (30cm)*

9 Mixed glazed ceramic; *14in (35cm) x 16in (40cm)*
10 Eggplant glazed pot; *21in (53cm) x 18in (45cm)*
11 Hand-thrown terracotta; *12in (30cm) x 18in (45cm)*
12 Gray glazed ceramic; *15in (37cm) x 16in (40cm)*
13 Dark blue glazed ceramic; *14in (35cm) x 10in (25cm)*
14 Latticework terracotta pot; *21in (53cm) x 18in (45cm)*
15 Pewter glazed terracotta; *24in (60cm) x 18in (45cm)*
16 Olive glazed terracotta; *30in (75cm) x 24in (60cm)*

17 Hand-thrown terracotta urn; *32in (80cm) x 24in (60cm)*
18 White crackle-glazed pot; *20in (50cm) x 24in (60cm)*
19 Black speckle-glazed pot; *18in (45cm) x 18in (45cm)*
20 Honey glazed pot; *15in (37cm) x 16in (40cm)*
21 Sage glazed pot; *21in (53cm) x 18in (45cm)*
22 Hand-thrown terracotta; *32in (80cm) x 32in (80cm)*
23 Slate gray glazed clay urn; *27in (68cm) x 14in (35cm)*

Wood

Containers made of wood make perfect partners for plants but need oil and preservative to extend their life.

Wood is an organic material, and when it comes in direct contact with moist potting mix, it will start to break down as a result of bacterial and fungal activity. Untreated softwood planters may only last up to a year, but softwood that has been pressure-treated during manufacture will last between ten and fifteen years. To extend the pot life and prevent staining, some of the more expensive tubs and boxes come with metal or plastic liners, which are a very good idea.

In contrast to other materials like stone, terracotta, and metal, containers made from wood are cheap and easy to construct yourself at home with limited woodworking skills. The advantage of this is that you can custom-build a container that will fit the space available, and be confident that it has the capacity for healthy plant growth. When the container is built, you can finish it in almost any color and style of decoration.

The wooden "Versailles-style" tub is a classic design well-suited to traditional and modern garden situations. To prolong the life of the container, empty it of plants and potting mix periodically and dry it out. Check the wood for signs of decay and treat the interior with a wood preservative.

PROTECTING WITH WOOD STAIN

Painted softwood containers are particularly susceptible to water damage at the joints and seams because they rarely have a chance to dry out completely once they have been planted. To avoid wood rot, it is a good idea to paint wooden boxes with a colored wood stain that contains preservative. Before you start, make sure the wood is dry and sound. If the wood has already been pressure-treated—by which I mean soaked with preservative under pressure by the timber supplier—then this extra coat will add even more protection. Always check that the preservative or paint you use is plant-friendly.

PROTECTING WOOD BY OILING

Untreated wood that is exposed to the sun will dry out and is prone to cracking. To limit this damage, feed the dry wood with linseed oil during the winter months when the box is clean and free of plant material. This linseed oil treatment will help preserve the wood and bring out the rich natural grain. Also, coat the interior with wood preservative to protect it when it comes in contact with the moist potting mix and thus extend its life.

A selection of wooden containers

Sizes are shown as *height* x *width*

1 Weathered pine trough; *8in (20cm) x 24in (60cm)*

2 Woven wicker basket; *10in (25cm) x 12in (30cm)*

3 Stained pine box; *17in (42cm) x 6in (15cm)*

4 Woven hazel basket; *8in (20cm) x 16in (40cm)*

5 Wooden barrel; *16in (40cm) x 18in (45cm)*

6 Wooden barrel; *16in (40cm) x 18in (45cm)*

7 Solid oak planter; *17in (42cm) x 17in (42cm)*

8 Stained wood box; *8in (20cm) x 4in (10cm)*

9 Teak outer liner; *23in (57cm) x 23in (57cm)*

10 Painted wood Versailles tub; *18in (45cm) x 18in (45cm)*

11 Solid oak planter with liner; *29in (72cm) x 29in (72cm)*

12 Weathered solid oak planter; *21in (53cm) x 21in (53cm)*

13 Blue wood-stained pine trough; *36in (90cm) x 12in (30cm)*

Stone

In container gardening, "stone" includes natural stone, terrazzo, concrete, and reconstructed stone.

Apart from natural stone, which has to be cut by machine or carved by hand, garden containers made from other stone-based materials can be formed in a mold, which allows for the mass production of many different sizes and shapes of pots at relatively low prices.

Reconstructed stone—which is simply stone "powder" bound with an adhesive—is used to make authentic-looking copies of traditional container shapes, like urns and pots mounted on pedestals. Some manufacturers, in an attempt to make their new pots look old and weathered, also use colored additives and surface coatings in the production process. Many contemporary containers, however, are available in simple square or cylinder shapes, and their appeal relies on the smooth matt surfaces and pale gray and white tones that reconstituted stone, concrete, and terrazzo finishes have to offer.

The tactile surface of this container made from textured stone compound provides a good foil to the black leaf color and smooth, fleshy feel of the Aeonium leaves.

AGING STONE CONTAINERS

To achieve an aged appearance, you need to establish the growth of algae and lichen on the pot surface. New pots, particularly those in sunny sites, present a hostile environment for these organisms to establish themselves. To encourage algal growth, you need to supply nutrients for the organisms to grow. Simply rub a fistful of lush, juicy grass across the pot surface. This green grass stain soon fades to brown. Other methods include brushing a layer of thinned natural yogurt over the pot surface or spraying on a liquid fertilizer. When treated, place your pots in a damp, shady site in long grass to create the ideal conditions for algae and lichen to flourish.

CLEANING STONE CONTAINERS

When planting containers, it is easy to spill potting mix and leave behind dirty finger marks on the pale stone surface. Most marks can be rubbed off when dry or washed off using soapy water and a plastic kitchen scourer. For stubborn stains, try using the type of abrasive pad used to rub down scratches on car body paint. If in any doubt about the effect this abrasive action will have on a smooth stone pot surface, check the result on a hidden area first.

A selection of stone containers

Sizes are shown as *height × width*

1 Tobacco terrazzo pot; *14in (35cm) × 14in (35cm)*
2 Pale gray terrazzo cylinder: *14in (35cm) × 16in (40cm)*
3 Reconstituted stone bowl; *12in (30cm) × 16in (40cm)*
4 White terrazzo trough *10in (25cm) × 12in (30cm)*
5 Black terrazzo pot *14in (35cm) × 18in (45cm)*
6 White terrazzo cylinder; *24in (60cm) × 14in (35cm)*
7 White terrazzo cylinder; *24in (60cm) × 8in (20cm)*
8 White terrazzo rectangle; *16in (40cm) × 24in (60cm)*
9 White terrazzo pot; *24in (60cm) × 24in (60cm)*

10 Candy twist concrete urn; *20in (50cm) × 16in (40cm)*
11 Stone pedestal urn; *18in (45cm) × 24in (60cm)*
12 Gray terrazzo cylinder; *36in (90cm) × 16in (40cm)*
13 Gray terrazzo trough: *14in (35cm) × 20in (50cm)*
14 Granite bowl; *8in (20cm) × 18in (45cm)*
15 White terrazzo square; *14in (35cm) × 14in (35cm)*

Metal

Casting, pressing, bending, and rolling are just some of the techniques used to make metal containers.

During manufacture, the surface of the metal can be treated by galvanizing, painting, powder-coating, and polishing to create a number of different matt and reflective finishes. This huge choice of effects makes metal a popular choice for the container gardener. Metal is also appealing because it is very durable and will survive outdoors with little or no maintenance. However, metal containers are not inert; galvanized surfaces will eventually lose their bright, shiny look and turn gray as the zinc oxidizes. Some steel containers designed with a rust finish can cause staining on light paving stones. To prevent this staining, make sure that water can drain away from the pot base. Some gardeners avoid metal containers because they think they conduct heat too efficiently, scorching the roots and drying out the potting mix, but in my experience, it never appears to have a harmful effect on the plants.

Powder-coated metal containers provide some of the most vividly colored pots available. Their brilliance is enhanced by their smooth, shiny finish and satisfying shapes. Some container manufacturers have stock colors and surface finishes and are also able to offer specific colors by special order.

PREVENTING RUST IN DRAINAGE HOLES

The big enemy of metal is rust. To protect against this, the manufacturers apply a zinc coating or galvanize the metal. Paint and powder coatings also offer protection. With all of these it is important not to damage the protective coating or the metal will corrode. However, sometimes plant containers are manufactured without drainage holes and you will need to drill holes into the pot base if the plants roots are to stay healthy. After drilling, reseal the broken metal surface with a protective coat of anti-rust paint. This will prevent the metal from rusting as water drains through the planting.

CLEANING POLISHED METAL CONTAINERS

Highly polished stainless steel or aluminum containers make a strong visual statement. To maintain the impact of their bright, reflective surface, you will need to keep the surface highly polished, using a window-cleaning spray and a soft cloth. Do not use abrasive scourers—they will scratch the surface. When watering the plants, be careful not to splash water or potting mix onto the polished metal. In hard-water areas, these splashes will leave behind white deposits of calcium, which can be rubbed off with a soft cloth. A regular application of a protective car wax repels water and makes polishing easier.

A selection of metal containers

Sizes are shown as height x width

1 Galvanized metal cylinder; *16in (40cm) x 12in (30cm)*
2 Galvanized metal vase; *15in (37cm) x 6in (15cm)*
3 Brushed stainless-steel; *20in (50cm) x 24in (60cm)*
4 Stainless-steel cube; *12in (30cm) x 12in (30cm)*
5 Recycled copper pot; *15in (37cm) x 16in (40cm)*
6 Stainless-steel pot; *16in (40cm) x 12in (30cm)*
7 Galvanized metal pot; *15in (37cm) x 6in (15cm)*
8 Recycled metal tub; *26in (65cm) x 16in (40cm)*

9 Rust-effect coated steel vase; *28in (70cm) x 17in (42cm)*
10 Galvanized metal bucket; *26in (65cm) x 24in (60cm)*
11 Blue powder-coated steel; *24in (60cm) x 48in (45cm)*
12 Red sprayed steel; *40in (1m) x 14in (36cm)*
13 Galvanized metal pot; *15in (37cm) x 16in (40cm)*
14 Twin-wall blued steel; *36in (90cm) x 24in (60cm)*
15 Recycled copper cylinder; *15in (37cm) x 8in (20cm)*
16 Aluminum pot; *40in (1m) x 16in (40cm)*

17 Galvanized metal cube; *18in (45cm) x 18in (45cm)*
18 Galvanized metal trough; *14in (35cm) x 36in (90cm)*
19 Lead planter; *16in (40cm) x 16in (40cm)*
20 Rust-effect coated steel; *24in (60cm) x 17in (42cm)*

Synthetic

*This category includes faux lead and terracotta pots
in traditional designs and more radical resin planters.*

One look at the selection of containers on display opposite shows you
how versatile polymers, plastics, fiberglass, and resins are and what creative
and imitative use they can be put to in container design. Virtually any size
or scale of container is now achievable in curvy or straight shapes, in
ridged, knobby, or smooth textures, or in matt or shiny metallic finishes.
What is so exciting for the container designer prepared to experiment with
these new materials is that the method of manufacture rarely limits the
shape or size of the container, and even large-scale planters are relatively
lightweight and inexpensive to produce. For those who prefer more
traditional styles, manufacturers of synthetic pots are also able to offer
extremely convincing copies of traditional lead, terracotta, and stone
container shapes. The advantages of the synthetic versions is that they
are cheaper as well as being frostproof and unbreakable.

*Unlimited by the constraints of
working with a natural material,
shapes of all sorts can be made using
synthetic materials and molds. Here,
a long trough has a wonderful
rounded shape. Its clean and shapely
lines are the perfect foil for the
rosettes of the succulent.*

CLEANING SYNTHETIC CONTAINERS

Potting mix stains and dirty handprints can be easily removed from most synthetic materials with
soapy water and a soft cloth. More stubborn marks may require the use of a kitchen scouring
pad, but try it out on a hidden area first if you are worried about damaging the surface. Be
careful to avoid scuffing or scratching plastic surfaces because once it is damaged, there is no
foolproof way of removing the marks.

LIGHTWEIGHT BENEFITS

A significant advantage of synthetic materials is their strength-to-weight ratio. The materials are
tough but lightweight. For this reason, large pots are easy to transport to any location, and they
are easy to put away if you are not using them. There are some very convincing lightweight
"rock" or "stone" containers that allow solid-looking pots and features to be used in places
such as balconies, roof gardens, or wooden deck areas where weight and transportation of
the pot to the site are often an issue.

A selection of synthetic containers

Sizes are shown as *height x width*

1   Faux stone square; *10in (25cm) x 10in (25cm)*
2   Faux copper pot; *16in (40cm) x 12in (30cm)*
3   White molded resin pot; *12in (30cm) x 13in (33cm)*
4   Faux lead square; *15in (37cm) x 15in (37cm)*
5   White molded resin trough; *7in (18cm) x 30in (75cm)*
6   Blue plastic container; *15in (37cm) x 18in (45cm)*
7   Faux cast iron pot; *15in (37cm) x 20in (50cm)*
8   Orange molded resin pot; *12in (30cm) x 13in (33cm)*
9   Faux lead trough; *8in (20cm) x 30in (75cm)*

10 Faux terracotta rectangle; *20in (50cm) x 16in (40cm)*
11 Gray molded resin planter; *12in (30cm) x 18in (45cm)*
12 Faux lead tub; *18in (45cm) x 16in (40cm)*
13 Gray molded resin planter; *18in (45cm) x 24in (60cm)*
14 Faux terracotta planter; *24in (60cm) x 26in (65cm)*
15 Faux carved stone bowl; *6in (15cm) x 14in (35cm)*
16 Faux terracotta tub; *20in (50cm) x 29in (73cm)*

container
principles

Choose healthy plants

Healthy and robust plants are the key to a successful container display. The plants need to look fantastic the moment they are planted, particularly when they are on display in a small area where they are will be subject to close scrutiny. Poor-quality specimens will not only detract from the appearance of the plantings but also slow the growth of the display and prevent it from filling out the container.

In a busy garden center the turnover of stock is quick enough for plants not to sit on the shelf long enough to deteriorate. Poorly maintained plants quickly show signs of neglect, overcrowding, poor nutrition, and disease. To avoid these problems, always buy from a source where the plants look well-tended and cared for. Plants that have been given space to grow rather than crowded together are likely to be in better health. Check the leaves for signs of pests and disease (*see page 146*) and do not be afraid to lift the plant out of its pot to inspect the health of its root system (*see opposite*). If there is a limited choice of plants available and the particular species you want for your display is of poor quality, it can usually be revived by routine pruning and feeding, but this will take time.

In containers, plants are grown in close proximity to one another and have to compete for nutrients and water. Give each container planting the best chance of survival by carefully selecting only good-quality, healthy plants.

WATCHPOINTS

1   *Healthy roots are important. Avoid plants with poor or overcrowded root systems. Young plants that have very recently been potted will not have an established root system, and if they are lifted out, the potting mix will fall away. Look for plants that are sufficiently established to hold the potting mix together but where the roots are not a solid mass up against the pot edge. Potbound plants are slower to establish when planted into your container because water cannot easily penetrate the root ball.*

3   *Tip the plant out of its pot and look for signs of grubs or insects that might be eating the roots.*

4   *It is better to buy a small, healthy-looking plant than a large, untidy one just because it has flowers. In the long term, the smaller one will grow and provide you with a better display.*

5   *Choose plants from the edge of a plant tray or display stand; these plants will have had access to more light and space to grow and should be more compact and sturdy.*

6   *Beware of trays of bedding plants where one or two plants are wilting. They may just be dry, but they may also be suffering from a root disease that will spread to the other plants in your container. A gentle tug will help you determine if their roots are sound.*

Signs of poor health

General poor condition

Avoid plants that do not look healthy on first appearance. On closer inspection, moss and weeds growing on the surface of the potting mix indicate that the plant has been in its pot for too long and is likely to be potbound and undernourished. Spots and speckles on the leaves or pieces eaten away may indicate damage from pests and diseases.

PLANTS PARTICULARLY PRONE INCLUDE:

Alyogyne

Buxus

Hedera varieties

Helichrysum

Tibouchina

Potbound roots

Check the roots of the plant before you buy it by lifting it out of its plastic container. A potbound plant with its roots packed in a tight mesh will take longer to establish itself in a container display than a plant whose roots can be seen just spreading into the potting mix around the edge of the pot.

PLANTS PARTICULARLY PRONE INCLUDE:

Agave americana

Aegopodium podagraria 'Variegata'

Chlorophytum comosum

Heuchera

Lamium 'Hermann's Pride'

Leymus arenarius

Yellowing leaves

These are a sign that the plant is undernourished or has root problems, because once the plant has used up all the nitrogen in its potting mix, it will carry nitrogen away from the older leaves to the younger ones, causing the older ones to turn yellow. Nitrogen is a vital element for the production of chlorophyll, the pigment that traps light energy for the plant.

PLANTS PARTICULARLY PRONE INCLUDE:

Anthemis punctata subsp. *cupaniana*

Asparagus densiflorus

Cordyline australis

Lotus maculatus

Petasites japonicus

Leggy stems

Plants need good light levels to grow, and if they do not have access to enough light, their stems will grow tall in an effort to reach the light source. This leads to straggly growth that is unable to physically support itself. The long stems are weak and are likely to break in windy weather. Very often these leggy stems also have softer growth and are prone to fungal attack.

PLANTS PARTICULARLY PRONE INCLUDE:

Argyranthemum varieties

Dahlia varieties

Kleinia senecioides

Melianthus major

Pelargonium tomentosum

Prepare containers for planting

Before planting a long-term container display, it is worth checking the pot over to make sure it is in good condition, particularly if it is going to stand outside all winter. Any cracks or chips in terracotta, ceramic, or stone-based materials can be filled with an epoxy resin to prevent the crack from spreading further and letting in water, which may lead to frost damage (*see page 148*). Long cracks in terracotta can be held together by copper wire "stitching" threaded through holes drilled on either side of the split, or the split can be patched inside with fiberglass matting.

Container cleaning

For many people, including myself, one of the main attractions of choosing terracotta as a container material is the color patina it develops with age. After several seasons outdoors, terracotta pots will accumulate layers of salts and algae on their surface. To prepare an old terracotta pot for planting, use a stiff brush and plenty of water and scrub it inside only. This will stop any pest or disease from a previous occupant from contaminating the new potting mix. Terrazzo containers can be scrubbed out with a kitchen scourer and water, while plastic pots can be prepared for planting with soapy water and a soft cloth to avoid any abrasive action that may damage the pot interior.

WORK SAFELY

If you are using a electric drill and an extension cord outdoors, do not let them get wet. Wear protective goggles while drilling and hammering to keep sharp chips of stone or metal from injuring your eyes. The newly formed drainage hole will have also sharp, rough edges.

Container drainage

Drilling holes in ceramic

Good drainage is absolutely essential to grow plants successfully in containers. Some pots intended as plant containers have no drainage hole in the base or have only a small, inadequate hole. To improve drainage, drill a large hole in their base. To do this:

◁ Turn the pot upside-down and, using an electric drill and a masonry bit, drill a series of small holes in the base. Drill them as close together as is practical.

▷ Using a hammer, carefully knock out the material between the holes to make one large single hole.

A small masonry drill bit is easier to use than a large-diameter bit. It puts less stress on the material and can prevent large cracks from forming and so prevent the pot from breaking.

Drilling holes in metal

◁ Mark your holes using a center punch or nail. Drill the hole using a large steel drill bit. Before you drill thin metals, place a block of wood under the metal surface to support it. For safety, hammer down sharp metal edges with a wooden dowel.

Adding materials for drainage

▷ The purpose of adding broken pot pieces or stones is to ensure the free passage of water through the potting mix to the drainage hole. Arrange the pieces over the hole so that you create as many cavities as possible. Larger curved pieces of broken terracotta pots are ideal for this.

Choose the right potting mix

The well-being of container-grown plants depends on the supply of light, nutrients, and water. Both nutrients and water are obtained via the potting mix, and different plants have different needs. The perfect growing conditions for each and every plant can be difficult to achieve in one pot, where, for example, you might have drought-tolerant succulents next to thirsty, leafy plants, yet it has always surprised me just how adaptable plants are. In my experience, as long as I use a free-draining potting mix that retains moisture well and has an "open" soil structure to allow oxygen to aerate the plant roots, then the plants will grow happily. The only plant species that will not grow in any type of potting mix are acid-loving plants such as Rhododendrons, Pieris, Calluna, and Restios.

Peat-based mix

This became the container gardening growing medium of choice for commercial growers and garden centers because of its ability to retain water and air. It is also light and easy to transport. Its major drawback is that it contains no nutrients, and all nutrients have to be added to the mix, making regular feeding or the use of controlled-release fertilizers essential. Also, peat-based potting mix can be difficult to rewet when it has dried out. Raw peat is naturally acidic, which makes it ideal as the base for ericaceous potting mix.

Coir-based mix

Produced from coconut waste, which is a renewable resource, coir-based mix was developed as an environmentally friendly alternative to peat. When first introduced, the properties of coir-based mix were not as impressive as other types, but they now have improved water retention, soil hygiene, and nutrition. Although nutrition and trace elements are present, liquid fertilizer needs to be applied regularly for best results with plants grown in this medium.

They require an acidic mix which is commonly known as ericaceous potting mix.

My preferred potting mix is loam-based and has about 20 percent organic matter added in the form of peat or coir fiber to help retain water. To keep the potting mix "open" and fully aerated, try not to firm down the mix when planting the display because this will drive air out and limit root growth. Here, we describe the merits and drawbacks of the four main potting mixes available to the container gardener to help you draw your own conclusions about which one is best for your planting needs.

Peat-free mix

As well as coir-based mix, there are several other peat-free alternatives available, made from ingredients like cocoa shells, sawdust, straw, woodchips, and bark. The last of these, bark, has been most studied and developed. It has established itself as an important and renewable ingredient in peat-free mix and is produced on a large scale. It is usually partially broken down by composting to help dissipate any harmful plant toxins before being made into potting mix. Its natural nutrient level is not high, so regular feeding of plants grown in bark is required.

Loam-based mix

This mix contains a high proportion of sterilized soil and is like buying good quality garden soil in a bag. Though there is a standard formula for loam- or soil-based mixes, the quality varies. In most cases, extra organic matter is needed to improve the soil structure and water-holding capacity. Plants in loam-based mix do not need regular feeding: this mix contains nutrients and tiny particles called colloids that help retain any nutrients that already exist in the soil. This soil is heavy, which can be useful for anchoring exposed plantings.

Reduce the weight of containers

In most garden sites, the weight and scale of a container planting only becomes an issue when the pot has to be transported to a new location, or placed on a balcony or roof terrace that can only carry a limited load. Whenever possible, try to move your pot to its final position before you plant it. The drainage material and potting mix dramatically increase the weight of the container; later, when the potting mix has been watered, the pot will become impossible to move. Trying to move a heavy pot not only puts strain on your back, but also risks damaging a large container that was probably quite expensive. Thin-walled ceramic pots are likely to crack, metal can bend, and the base of a ceramic or resin pot may chip it is if rocked when full.

Halving pot weight

One way to keep down the overall weight of a large container planting is to use a lightweight potting mix. Loam-based potting mixes are the heaviest, so opt for a peat-, coir-, or bark-based mix instead. Alternatively, you can reduce the total volume of potting mix used in the planting by only filling half the pot with soil and padding out the rest with a lightweight material. My technique involves a two-stage approach. First, I place an empty, upturned plastic pot inside the large container to fill the internal space. Then I fill in around the plastic pot with drainage gravel. Only one-third of the space is then left to fill with potting mix. When trying to reduce the weight of a container, bear in mind that for plantings intended to last for several years, the more potting mix there is in a container, the healthier the plants will be. Any excessive reduction in potting mix volume may damage plant health.

Step 1

A large, round pot can be rolled along on its base rather than picked up. When rolling terracotta or ceramics on hard surfaces, be careful not to chip the base. Get help when lifting large pots, or use a hand truck.

Step 2

Find a large plastic pot that fits upside-down inside your pot. It is likely to make a watertight seal when wedged in place, so cut V-shaped notches in the rim with pruners to allow for drainage.

Step 3

Make sure there is at least 12–14 n (30–35 cm) from the rim down to the plastic pot to allow for a suitable depth of potting mix for plant growth. A layer of gravel or lightweight beads will help keep the drainage holes clear of potting mix.

Step 4

Fill the container with potting mix. Peat-, coir-, or bark-based mixes are lighter than loam-based mixes.

Other weight reducers

Lightweight ceramic beads

This aggregate, made from expanded balls of clay, has an open, honeycomb-like structure and is both tough and lightweight. Ceramic beads are able to absorb water and so provide a small reserve of moisture and nutrients. Because of these beneficial properties, a higher proportion of ceramic beads to potting mix can be used to fill a container to keep its weight down.

Moving containers

Container stands on wheels

Sooner or later, you will need to move a large, full container, either to change your display or to move your plants to a frost-free site for winter. One simple method is to use a low wooden platform on casters. Tip the pot back to slip the platform under the pot base. As long as you have a hard surface to run the pot along, these stands on wheels make moving very easy.

Styrofoam

Chunks of broken-up styrofoam will help bulk out the interior of a pot with virtually no weight gain. Although you are creating a second use for this waste product, styrofoam is not biodegradable and will sit in the base of the pot forever, so try to keep its use to a minimum.

Hand trucks

A hand truck is easiest to use if its platform can be placed under a tilted pot with no lifting. An old blanket will protect the pot surface from scratches in transit. Alternatively, a low-cost solution is to slide a sheet of heavy-duty polythene under your pot and then drag the sheet along the ground, bringing the pot with you. This method does the least damage to a full and spreading planting.

Plant for success

There are dozens of combinations and styles that can be achieved when planting container displays. There are no set rules, and I would encourage you to experiment with your own design ideas and not to let minor setbacks put you off. The following step-by-step method is intended to show you the basic skills in planting a large traditional-style pot where one tall feature plant is surrounded by a mix of smaller flower and foliage plants. Knowing the different growth rates, heights, and spreads of your plant selection helps to produce a well-proportioned display. With less familiar plants, however, this understanding only comes with experience, since plants do not always behave as described on their label, and one may thrive in a container setting while another may fail.

Step 1

Work out your planting plan To establish a design, I think it is easiest to work with the actual plants. Keep them in their plastic pots and arrange them on the surface of the potting mix so that you get a visual idea of how they will all fit together in the display. Once you are happy with the effect, arrange the plants in the same pattern on the ground, and then, one by one, lift them out of their pots and plant them.

Step 2

Work from the middle of the display Establish your central feature plant and then work out from this point, planting your tallest growers first and gradually moving down the scale to your shortest. Plant in a systematic way so that plants of the same type are evenly spaced across the pot surface.

Planting tips

1   Water all plants well before adding them to the display.
     Soak in a bucket of water any that are particularly dry.

2   Keep the soil structure "open" and aerated and do not
     over-firm the potting mix around the plants.

4   Do not worry about creating symmetrical patterns, since
     they will be blurred as the planting grows up.

5   Consider which side your planting design will be viewed
     from so you do not waste plants.

6   Put inexpensive bedding plants, such as Lobelia,
     among your main players to cover the potting mix
     before the larger plants develop. Though the bedding
     plants will be hidden when the planting matures, they
     offer a degree of interest during the early stages.

7   Arrange the longest trailing stems so that they face
     inward rather than outward—covering the potting
     mix will make the display look more established.

Step 3

Positioning small plants Even though some plants are small,
I always try to use them to best effect in an arrangement. To
achieve this, I often tilt the plant on its side so that its best
foliage or flowers face out toward the rim of the pot. Some of
the root ball may be left exposed on the soil surface, but as long
as it is kept moist, the plant will thrive.

Step 4

Filling out for a full effect Once you have finished planting,
add some more potting mix to fill the container to about 1 in
(2.5 cm) below the rim. Take a look at your finished efforts to
see, even at this early stage of plant growth, if the arrangement
looks balanced. Reposition plants if you need to. When you are
satisfied, water the display thoroughly.

Maintain plants regularly

A container planting should really be treated just like a garden, but on a smaller scale. It requires the same amount of attention as your favorite flower border if you want it to look its best all year.

Each pot is only capable of holding a limited amount of soil and water to sustain the plants, so the nutrients in the soil and water need replenishing on a regular basis during the growing season to promote healthy leaf growth and flower production. As the season progresses, there are regular maintenance tasks to perform. The spent flowers will need deadheading, and trailing stems and vigorous plants in containers need trimming back so that they do not overwhelm the other plants in the display or the pot and ruin the balanced appearance of the display.

Soil compaction

Preventing soil compaction

The regular pounding effect of water on the potting mix surface creates a hard outer crust that prevents water and air from penetrating this top layer. Not surprisingly, loam-based potting mixes (*see page 136*) are more prone to compaction than soilless mixes. Ways to avoid the problem involve dissipating the force of the water by watering onto another hard surface (*see below*), onto a stone or bark mulch, or sinking a small flower pot into the potting mix and watering into that.

Opening up the soil structure

Once the soil has become compacted, it needs to be broken up. For large pot surfaces, use a hand fork or, for smaller pots, a kitchen fork or piece of stick. In mature plantings, the potting mix surface can also be bound up by roots. Use a hand fork to ease the roots apart and allow water to penetrate more easily. Alternatively, repot large plantings (*see page 152*), remove the top layer of roots and potting mix, and replace with new mix to free up the soil structure.

Deadheading

By preventing old flowers from setting seed, deadheading promotes the formation of new flowers. Picking off spent flowers also prevents them from falling back into the display and rotting, which, in turn, rots the plant stems and foliage. This is a problem for Begonias and Pelargoniums and especially Regal Pelargoniums.

Some plants need to be deadheaded purely for cosmetic reasons. For example, I always remove the lower, spent flowers of Canna because they detract from the rest of the display. With Argyranthemum, I shear off all the flowers at once to encourage a beautiful second flush of color.

PLANTS THAT NEED DEADHEADING

Anthemis	Osteospermum
Begonia	Pelargonium
Canna	Petunia
Dahlias	Solenostemon
Nicotiana	Verbena

Feeding

Plants grown in the confines of a container have a restricted root run and therefore limited access to nutrients. In crowded containers, there is a higher-than-usual plant density, and the supply of nutrients in the potting mix is quickly exhausted. Controlled-release fertilizer pellets mixed into the potting mix at planting time will provide a steady supply of food to your plants to sustain them. These fertilizers in pellet form are also available to buy as pellet clusters, designed to be pushed into the surface of the potting mix immediately after planting. A reliable way of providing instant nutrition is to water the plants with a soluble powdered fertilizer every two weeks (*see right*); this way, you can adjust the amount or frequency of feeding and respond quickly to your plants' needs.

Cut back trailing stems

It is unlikely that all the plants within your display are of equal vigor, so some management of the more vigorous ones is necessary if they are not to overwhelm the lesser plants. Climbers and scrambling plants whose nature it is to climb over and smother their neighbors are usually the main culprits. Keep their growth in check by regular pinching out and pruning, but always keep the overall shape and balance of the display in mind when cutting back. This may mean only cutting out some of the unruly shoots and leaving a few climbing strands to make their way through your feature plant.

Trimming back foliage is all part of the ongoing maintenance of a planting and can be compared to the regular tasks you carry out in the garden, such as weeding flower beds, tying in, pruning, and staking stems, without which the garden looks out of control. Take time to stand back from your container and assess the overall planting design. Be prepared to cut out shoots that are growing in the wrong place or support lanky stems with canes if this improves the visual appeal.

Step 1: remove untidy growth

If you create the ideal conditions for your container-grown plants, it can lead to exceptional growth that needs to be trained in the right direction or pruned back. This *Helichrysum petiolare* threatens to engulf the palm in the center, and because the effectiveness of the planting relies on a balance between the two, I am trimming it back and removing its yellow flowers, which I dislike.

Step 2: reshaping the display

The aim when reshaping a planting is to remove enough growth to restore a balance to the design, but in such a way that it appears as if little has been altered. To achieve this, cut back stems to a side shoot or take out whole shoots completely. When cutting back thick shoots, cut the stem at a downward angle to hide the cut ends, since these often turn white and look unattractive.

TRAILING PLANTS THAT MAY NEED CUTTING BACK

Bidens ferulifolia

Dichondra 'Silver Falls'

Geranium 'Anne Folkard'

Hedera varieties

Helichrysum petiolare

Kleinia senecioides

Lamium galeobdolon 'Hermann's Pride'

Lotus berthelotii

Lotus maculatus

Lysimachia nummularia 'Aurea'

Osteospermum jucundum

Pelargonium tomentosum

Petunia trailing varieties

Plectranthus ciliatus

Plectranthus madagascariensis

Plectranthus zatarhendii

Tropaeolum majus

Train pot-grown climbers

Rather than relying on one large central plant for height in your display, consider using climbing plants. If the structural support itself is elegant, it can even provide some interest before the climber becomes established.

There are a range of supports available, including garden canes, plastic "sticks," metal spirals, wood or metal trellises, and also simple metal rods that can be used on their own or to create a wigwam structure. I prefer to use natural hazel sticks cut from a coppiced tree in my own yard. In my opinion, their less-than-uniform shape adds to the charm of a planting. Their rough, natural surface is ideal for climbers of all types to cling to, be they twining plants such as *Thunbergia alata* or plants with grasping petioles or tendrils like *Rhodochiton atrosanguineus*. Ordinary shrub prunings can also be effective as natural canes if carefully selected.

When tying plants to smooth bamboo garden canes, first tie the garden string to the cane just above a node and wrap it around the node at least two times. This will prevent the fastening from slipping.

Avoid smooth canes

Metal rods and spirals make very stylish supports when trying to create a modern planting, but they are not actually very useful as plant supports. Their metal surface is so smooth and shiny that they offer very little for the young plants to cling to, and any attempt to tie plants to them with string usually ends with the whole works just slipping down into a pile at the bottom of the poles.

Encouraging young stems

Most climbers will eventually start climbing the support you have given them, but to speed the process, carefully tie the stems of young plants to the canes. By first tying the string to the support and then tying a loose knot around the stem, you avoid damaging tender young stems while allowing room for the stem to thicken as the plant matures.

CLIMBERS FOR GROWING IN CONTAINERS

Aconitum helmsleyanum

Clematis varieties

Cobaea scandens

Eccremocarpus scaber

Hedera varieties

Ipomoea lobata and *I. tricolor*

Lapageria rosea

Lathyrus odoratus

Maurandya barclayana

Passiflora varieties

Plumbago auriculata

Rhodochiton atrosanguineus

Senecio macroglossus 'Variegata'

Sollya heterophylla

Thunbergia alata

Tropaeolum peregrinum and *T. tuberosum*

Tweedia caerulea

Combat common pests and diseases

If you were to take a look at the extensive list of pests and diseases that could affect your container plants, you might be discouraged from gardening altogether. In theory, within the confined space of a pot, a disease will quickly infect all the inhabitants, but in reality, if the plants are healthy to start with, they will have the natural resources to fend off attack and few diseases will cause irreversible damage. Check your plantings daily for any signs of ill health and always take swift action. Where possible, I have chosen to feature plants (*see pages 26-115*) that are known for their reliability when grown in containers and their resistance to pests and diseases. Any plant species that need special care to keep them in good health are noted in the Plant Directory (*see pages 154-185*).

Slugs and snails

Typical damage is irregular holes chewed in leaves, but if there is no sign of a slime trail, suspect some other pest. Chemical deterrents usually contain aluminum sulfate or metaldehyde. Nonchemical means include slug traps baited with beer that the creatures fall into and drown. To protect individual pots, wrap a copper barrier tape around the pot. I also check my pots in the evening and pick off any slugs or snails that I see.

PLANTS PARTICULARLY AT RISK INCLUDE:

Hostas

Cannas

Dahlias

Eucomis

Impatiens

Ipomoea batatas 'Blackie'

Viola

Aphids

These prolific creatures are the bane of gardeners and, encouraged by warm weather, they multiply rapidly. Depending on the time of year, there are both winged and flightless adults. They attack the soft growing tips of plants, often causing distortion of leaves and the destruction of flower buds. Chemical aphid sprays are available, but for small infestations, it is often more effective to pinch out the damaged tips.

PLANTS PARTICULARLY AT RISK INCLUDE:

Argyranthemum

Dahlia

Fatsia japonica

Helichrysum petiolare

Verbena

Viola

Vine weevil

This pest likes containers, possibly because the sterilized potting mix contains none of its natural enemies. The brown-headed, white, C-shaped grubs feed on roots from late summer to late spring, causing wilting and death. The adults are flightless beetles that chew unsightly but not fatal notches in leaf edges (*seen in picture on large leaf*). Watering in parasitic nematodes once the potting mix has warmed up helps limit damage.

PLANTS PARTICULARLY AT RISK INCLUDE:

Aeonium

Begonia

Echeveria

Euonymus 'Emerald 'n' Gold'

Heuchera

Pelargonium

Prevention

Trying to keep your plants free from pests and diseases is easier than trying to eradicate an established outbreak.

It is impossible to completely stop pests and diseases from establishing themselves on your plants, but resistance can be encouraged by growing strong, robust plants free from the weakening effects of drought or poor nutrition that make them prone to attack.

Insect populations can build very quickly, particularly in warm weather, so it is essential to make regular inspections and then act quickly to treat the first sign of disease or insect attack. Seek out the pests and remove them by spraying, rubbing, or wiping off the culprits, or simply prune out the affected part. Do not put infected prunings on the compost pile. Burn them so that they do not have an opportunity to reinfect the planting.

In a large and full planting, infestations of insect pests can go unnoticed until they are out of control. Check the growing tips and the undersides of the leaves regularly, since they are the most likely places to harbor pests. Hairy or scented leaves, such as those of Pelargonium *'Lady Plymouth' shown above, are usually less prone to insect attack.*

WATCHPOINTS

1   *Insects seek shelter on the undersurface of the leaf and are often concentrated around the main leaf veins, where food is plentiful. Examine the plants carefully because many insects are well-camouflaged—green caterpillars are easy to miss and aphids can tuck themselves into the young, rolled-up leaves of plants like Canna. Rub or wipe off the insects and eggs.*

2   *Wet foliage encourages the spread of fungal diseases, so be careful when watering. This is particularly true of dense, fleshy foliage such as Begonias.*

3   *Leaving spent flowers lying on top of foliage encourages rot. Regular deadheading or picking over will help to avoid rot as well as keeping the display looking neat.*

4   *Be aware that overfeeding container plantings with high-nitrogen fertilizer can promote growth that is soft and prone to disease, creating an easy target for sap-sucking insects.*

5   *Act quickly! Scientific estimates suggest that in one season, if conditions are ideal, a single aphid could theoretically give rise to several thousand tons of aphids if all its offspring survived.*

6   *Potting mixes are available with systemic insecticides. These are taken up by the plants, giving them long-term protection against a wide range of pests and diseases. Do not use systemic insecticides if you are growing culinary herbs or food crops.*

Protect pots and plant roots

The main enemy of container plantings, and modern clay pots in particular, is freezing weather conditions. We cannot control the weather, but we can limit its damaging effects on plants and vulnerable pots, especially during the winter months, by taking preventative measures.

The damage caused to pots is the result of wet potting mix freezing inside the terracotta container. As the water freezes, it expands, pushing upward. If the pot has a narrow neck, it is likely to crack and then break apart under the pressure. Lining pots with air-filled wrapping material will act as a buffer when the potting mix expands. Storing clay pots indoors when not in use is also a good idea. This will keep moisture from seeping into cracks, freezing, and causing the pot surface to flake away.

Signs of frost damage

The quality and thickness of a terracotta pot will determine how resistant it is to frost damage. Machine-made pots are more prone to splitting and shaling than hand-thrown pots, where the container has been worked into shape out of a single block of clay. Still in use today are some hundred-year-old clay pots that have been left outside every winter—testament to the durability of quality handmade containers.

Lining pots

When the potting mix expands and solidifies in freezing weather, pots at risk from frost damage can be lined with plastic air-filled sheets. This protective lining works because each air bubble gets squashed against the pot interior to absorb the expansion, and then re-forms as the air temperature rises and the potting mix softens. With big, valuable pots, I use large, air-filled plastic envelopes originally used for packing fragile items for shipping, placed in the middle of the potting mix.

Protect tender plants

Many fast-growing tender perennials are inexpensive, so the cost of overwintering them in a heated greenhouse, particularly in cold areas, cannot be justified. It makes better financial sense to buy new stock each year. However, large specimens or more unusual plants are harder to replace and are worth bringing in under glass to protect them from extreme cold and frost.

Other tender plants, such as Melianthus, Canna, and Dahlias, can be cut down, dug up, and stored as dormant plants in a well-ventilated garage. In this state, they need no light but should be kept cool, frost-free, and just moist through the winter.

All tender plants should be kept dry in cold temperatures to prevent root rot and to concentrate the sap to form a natural "antifreeze."

Wrapping tender plants in fleece

Plants that are borderline hardy in your zone can often be left outside in winter if they are given protection during particularly cold spells. Use straw, burlap, or bubble wrap as insulation. Wrap this around the pot and the plant, but be aware this is not a permanent solution. To shelter tall foliage plants such as Cordyline and Phormium against the effects of cold winds, wrap up the plants in several layers of horticultural fleece—again, this is only for emergency use.

Moving tender plants indoors

Tender evergreen plants can be lifted out of their containers, potted, and brought into the shelter of a greenhouse or conservatory before the first frosts. Plants like Aeonium, Agave, Cordyline, Plectranthus, Solenostemon, Abutilon, Aspidistra, Kalanchoe, and Echeveria make dramatic indoor specimens before being moved back outside the next summer. If space is short, take cuttings in late summer and overwinter smaller plants; they will grow quickly the following spring.

Keep potting mix moist

Growing plants in containers is a creative and fun form of gardening, but it has one major drawback: the plants have to be watered and, in summer, this can mean twice a day. With just one or two pots that sit outside the back door, this is an easy job, but if the containers are arranged around a large garden or you have a huge number of them, then watering becomes a major chore. Running out the length of hose or walking back and forth to the faucet with a watering can be very time-consuming. There are ways to make this job easier and quicker; these are outlined below.

A good tip to remember when watering pots is to always water from the back and try not to water in the same spot each time, since this can create a hole in the plant material that ruins the effect.

Automatic watering

Auto-irrigation systems

This involves setting up a simple irrigation system in which each pot is fed by one or more capillary tubes from an outside water supply. Care is needed in regulating flow so as not to flood or deprive your pots. It can be operated manually or by an automatic timing device that irrigates the pots at preset times. This system does not take into account the moisture in the soil, but more sophisticated systems will. In hard-water areas, make sure the nozzles do not become blocked.

Capillary method

This low-tech method will water pots while the water supply in the receptacle lasts. Simply place a full bucket of water or a watering can above the level of your pot. Attach one end of a strip of wet greenhouse capillary matting to your vessel of water and place the other end in the potting mix. Water will flow out of the vessel and down to your pot until the vessel is empty. Some experimentation may be needed to establish the right thickness of strip to create a steady drip rate.

Retaining moisture

Mulches

A decorative covering of pebbles, stone chips, or glass not only looks attractive but keeps the potting mix moist and preserves water by reducing evaporation from the soil surface. This is useful when growing large single specimens, such as Japanese Acers, that enjoy cool, moist roots. Mulches also prevent dirty soil splashes on the pot and plant during watering.

Water-retaining crystals

These can be added to the soil to provide a reserve of moisture for the roots should the soil become dry, and for this reason they are useful in hanging baskets, which tend to dry out quickly. Blend the potting mix and dry crystals together, then water thoroughly. Take care not to add too many or the expanding crystals will push themselves and the soil out of the pot.

Environmental issues

Water is a precious resource and, if your supply is metered, a costly commodity. For this reason, as much use should be made of collected rainwater as possible. Rainwater is also essential for irrigating acid-loving plants in hard-water areas. Careful watering of each individual container with a watering can or hose is also far more economical than using a sprinkler.

Set up your irrigation system carefully to maximize water use and minimize runoff. Before you install the system, make sure it complies with all relevant building codes. In many municipalities, you must fit an anti-siphon valve between your water supply and the irrigation system. This is to protect household water from being contaminated if dirty water is sucked back into the system.

Know when to repot

Plants grown in pots over a long period of time will produce an expansive root system that exhausts the potting mix of nutrients. The roots also make it difficult for oxygen to penetrate the soil, as they tend to choke up every pore of the soil.

Regular repotting supplies fresh nutrients, opens up the soil structure, and so promotes new root growth. The signs that indicate when a plant is in desperate need of repotting include:

- Poor growth and yellowed leaves.
- The plant wilts more quickly than well-potted specimens and needs constant watering.
- The surface of the potting mix is matted with a web of roots.
- When lifted out of the pot, potbound plants reveal a solid mass of roots pressed against the pot.

Step 1

Large plants in big pots can be extremely heavy and are often reluctant to come out of their pots. Tip the pot on its side so that you do not have to lift the weight of the potting mix, and to get a better grip on the plant. A stubborn plant might need two people—one to hold the pot, the other to pull out the plant. If the plant is stuck, give it a thorough watering to help release the roots' grip on the side of the pot, or run a long-bladed knife around the inside of the pot to free up the root ball.

Step 2

Once the root ball is free, tease out the roots from the potting mix and shake off most of the old soil. Loosen the root ball by rubbing the roots through your fingertips to separate out the matted strands. Use a strong jet of water from a hose to wash out the soil stuck between the roots.

1   *When potting plants for long-term displays, use a pot with a smooth interior to make it easier to remove the plant at a later date.*

2   *Avoid using pots whose neck is a smaller than their body. Otherwise, the plant will be impossible to remove without breaking the pot apart.*

3   *Planting the display inside a pot liner is a good idea for large specimens like large clipped topiary. This way the pot exterior is just an outer jacket and the plant can be pulled out in its liner through a side panel that comes off. This takes much less effort than lifting an established plant out of a container.*

Step 3

Up to one-third of the roots can be cut off. Cut through a few of the thicker roots and remove whole sections. Keep the finer roots intact, since these are useful to help reestablish the plant. The dirt and grit around the roots will damage the blades of your pruners, so use an old or cheap pair.

Step 4

Replace the drainage material in the pot base and put a layer of potting mix on top. Position the pared-down root ball and fill in around it with fresh, dry potting mix. Push the soil around the root ball, and then shake the plant and pot to make sure that potting mix settles in any gaps. Do not firm down the soil. Water thoroughly and keep the planting out of hot sunshine and drying winds for several weeks while the roots reestablish themselves.

container
plant directory

In this directory are plants that have become, over time, personal favorites and, perhaps just as important, plants that are easy to grow as long as their basic needs are satisfied. When well-grown, they are generally pest- and disease-resistant. Plant height dimensions can be misleading for the container gardener, who is often using differently sized immature plants that bear no relation to the full height of the mature plant, so I have omitted them unless relevant. Use the container portrait dimensions *(see pages 26–115)* as a guide to the size of plants used.

A

Abutilon 'Kentish Belle'

An open and arching shrub with considerable grace. The foliage is sparse, making the flowers easily seen. They show up well against their dark, wiry stems. **Cultivation** It needs canes to support its lax stems to give height if used as a container centerpiece. Sun/light shade. **Hardiness** Tolerates a few degrees of frost, but is best kept above freezing during the winter.

See page 70

Abutilon 'Nabob'

An erect, evergreen shrub with large maplelike leaves and heavy, somber-looking, nodding flowers. Ideal as a center plant in a display. **Cultivation** It is potentially a large shrub, but it tolerates pruning and can be kept to a manageable size. Late-summer cuttings produce vigorous plants for use the following summer. Sun. **Hardiness** Stands occasional winter temperatures as low as 32°F (0°C). A temperature of 50°F (10°C) will keep it flowering throughout the year.

See page 44

Adiantum capillus-veneris

A useful fern for providing soft texture among harder and shinier plants. Its wiry, black stems are a feature that should be exploited. **Cultivation** Keep out of full sun and drying winds. Shearing off the foliage in spring will promote a sprouting of fresh new fronds. **Hardiness** Tolerates some cold, but loses its leaves below freezing, and is best kept at 41°F (5°C) or above.

See page 48

Aegopodium podagraria 'Variegatum'

This herbaceous perennial is an ornamental variety of an invasive weed. It is only slightly less vigorous than its weedy counterpart, and a pot is the safest place for it. It is valuable for its good, clean, cream-white variegation. **Cultivation** In spring, it bears fluffy white flowers. Cut them off to prevent them from seeding and detracting from the foliage. Sun or shade. **Hardiness** Zones 4–9.

See page 102

Aeonium arboreum

A tender succulent with thick, branching, woody stems that bear fleshy terminal rosettes. **Cultivation** An easily cared-for plant whose rosettes root easily if they are cut off just below the leaves and pushed into a gritty potting mix that is kept just moist. Sun or light shade. **Hardiness** Give a winter minimum of 46–50°F (8–10°C).

See page 76

Aeonium 'Zwartkop'

This is one of the most dramatic plants available for small-scale container gardening. **Cultivation** Tolerant of a wide range of conditions, growing well in the same pot alongside such unlikely companions as *Begonia rex*. Give it plenty of light. Be brave and cut back leggy plants. They will shoot from below the cut. In hard-water areas, keep water splashes off the foliage. **Hardiness** Give a winter minimum of 46–50°F (8–10°C).

See page 32

Agastache 'Apricot Sprite'

The subtle mix of colors provided by the stems, buds, flowers, and foliage make this a plant of great value for restrained color themes. **Cultivation** Keep potting mix on the dry side to get the most intense color from the gray-green foliage. Sun. **Hardiness** In well-drained potting mix, this has withstood freezing temperatures in my garden, but for guaranteed survival, offer frost protection; otherwise, treat it as an annual.

See page 28

Agave americana 'Variegata'

A dramatic plant for the container gardener. It makes a robust rosette of thick, fleshy leaves armed with spines along their edges. **Cultivation** Can reach 6 ft (2 m) or more in height, but its growth is slowed in a pot and it can be kept small for several years. Give it plenty of sun and good drainage. **Hardiness** Withstands the occasional frost but is happier with a winter minimum of between 41° and 46°F (5°–8°C).

See page 76

Anthemis punctata subsp. cupaniana

This is an evergreen perennial plant valued for its silvery filigree foliage and freely produced flowers. It has a vigorous spreading habit, ideal for spilling out of pots. **Cultivation** Neaten up the plant by shearing off the first flush of flowers when they are over. More flowers will be produced. Sun. **Hardiness** Though hardy in Zones 6–9, it dislikes wet and cold, so provide exceptionally good drainage to help it through the winter.

See page 58

Antirrhinum (Luminaire Series)™ 'Trailing White'

White is eye-catching and can be a distraction, but this Antirrhinum presents its color in a way that blends into a planting. Its trailing habit and soft foliage make it a favorite. Regular deadheading helps promote a continuous show of flowers. **Cultivation** Treat as a half-hardy annual and sow in gentle heat in late winter or early spring. Sun, light shade. **Hardiness** It flowers up to the first hard frost.

See page 54

Antirrhinum (Luminaire Series)™ 'Deep Trailing Yellow'

The flowers of this trailing snapdragon have a charm and lightheartedness that lifts and refreshes a planting. Flowers come in flushes, but there are always flowers on the plant and they are produced over a long season. **Cultivation** and **Hardiness** Treat it the same as Antirrhinum 'Trailing White'.

See page 70

Alocasia sanderiana

A tender evergreen with striking leaves that add a touch of the tropical to a display. In ideal conditions, the leaves grow to 12–16 in (30–40 cm) long, but outdoors in a container they are often much smaller. **Cultivation** It needs warm summers and sheltered conditions to succeed outdoors. Keep it out of direct sun and drying winds. **Hardiness** A minimum of 59°F (15°C) is required to see this Alocasia safely through the winter.

See page 114

Aloe ferox

This is an all-over prickly succulent with lots of character. Mature plants reach 6 ft (2 m) in height, but young plants make ideal architectural specimens for planting in a pot on their own. **Cultivation** Give it plenty of light, especially in winter. Sun. **Hardiness** It needs a winter temperature of around 50°F (10°C) and fairly dry potting mix.

See page 76

Alyogyne huegelii

The straggly, open habit and sparse foliage of this evergreen shrub have little to commend them, but the flowers are of outstanding beauty. The silky blue petals unfurl into large, saucerlike flowers. Set it among plants whose foliage is stronger and enjoy the flowers. **Cultivation** Pinching out shoot tips at the start of the season will encourage bushiness and greater numbers of flowers. Sun. **Hardiness** Protect from frost.

See page 62

Argyranthemum foeniculaceum

A shrubby plant ideal for a frothy summer effect. The gray-green foliage is finely cut and the long-stalked flowers are produced nonstop throughout the summer. **Cultivation** Late-summer cuttings root easily and can be overwintered as small plants that grow quickly in spring. Pinch out growing tips to encourage bushiness. Benefits from regular deadheading. Sun. **Hardiness** Withstands the first few light frosts but needs winter protection.

See page 110

Askiodiosperma paniculatum

This belongs to the Restionaceae family, whose members are commonly known as Restios. This is a dwarf species that only grows to around 24 in (60 cm). It makes a very good architectural container specimen. **Cultivation** Must have nonalkaline potting mix and be watered with soft water—rainwater is ideal. Sun. **Hardiness** It will withstand moderate frost, but in a container it is better kept frost-free during winter.

See page 92

Asparagus densiflorus

Many common houseplants make good container plants. This is one of them. It is perfect for filling in around the base of a planting to cover the bare potting mix when the planting is young. **Cultivation** An easily cared-for plant, but avoid dry conditions and scorching sun. Shade. **Hardiness** Treat it as a houseplant during the winter and plant out when all danger of frost has passed.

See page 64, 98

Aspidistra elatior

Despite being an old-fashioned and much-derided plant, the Aspidistra is a very useful foliage plant whose long and broad leaves can be used as major structural elements in a planting. **Cultivation** Keep moist and out of direct sunlight and strong drying winds. Shade. **Hardiness** Although usually grown as a houseplant, *Aspidistra elatior* is tougher than you might imagine and will survive temperatures a few degrees below freezing.

See page 64

Athyrium filix-femina 'Frizelliae'

This is an unusual deciduous fern with lobed leaflets that create all sorts of zigzag patterns and ruffs along their arching stems. It has a neatness and charm that never fails to draw attention. As with all ferns, there is great beauty in the unfurling fronds in spring. **Cultivation** Providing it is kept moist, this fern tolerates both shade and full sun. **Hardiness** Zones 4–9.

See page 90

Athyrium niponicum var. pictum

This is one of my top ten plants. The foliage has the most subtle combinations of colors, with silvery gray, pink-purple, and green blended together so delicately. Leaf color varies, so select a good form when you are buying. **Cultivation** It grows better in a neutral to acidic potting mix. Keep moist and out of hot sunshine. Shade. **Hardiness** Zones 5–8.

See page 90

Begonia 'Comtesse de Montesquieu'

Begonias with large and ornamental foliage (usually hybrids of *Begonia rex*) are much underused as container plants. The range of colors is wide, and both leaves and stems often have a hairy or dimpled texture. **Cultivation** Do not plant out until all danger of frost has passed and the overnight low temperature is at least 48–50°F (9–10°C). Prevent water from getting into the crown. Shade. **Hardiness** A minimum temperature of 50°F (10°C) is required.

See page 106

Begonia 'Fire Flush'

The remarkably colored leaves of 'Fire Flush' are held on stems covered in intensely red, dense hairs. Pale pink flowers are produced late in the season but do little to improve the appearance of the plant and are best removed. **Cultivation** and **Hardiness** as for *B.* 'Comtesse de Montesquieu'.

See page 106

Begonia 'Fireworks'

'Fireworks' is one of the most dramatically colored foliage begonias. Its multicolored leaves make it an ideal specimen for use on its own, but it also works well with a wide range of colors, including pinks, whites, silver, and primrose yellow.

Cultivation and **Hardiness** as for *B.* 'Comtesse de Montesquieu'.

See page 94

B

Bacopa 'White Suttis 98'

This is a plant with tiny flowers and foliage but a big impact. It grows in dense mats that spill out of pots, and it flowers from spring until the first frost. Other Bacopa varieties include pink and lavender-colored forms and a variegated variety. **Cultivation** Easily grown and recovers well from the occasional drying out. **Hardiness** Treat as a tender annual.

See page 52

Begonia 'Connie Boswell'

A tall variety with long leaf stems and open growth. **Hardiness** and **Cultivation** as for *B.* 'Comtesse de Montesquieu'.

See page 94

Begonia 'Martin Johnson'

Another Begonia with outstanding foliage. The deeply cut leaves with jagged margins give it added drama. **Cultivation** and **Hardiness** as for *B.* 'Comtesse de Montesquieu'.

See page 94

Begonia 'Peace'

Given good growing conditions, the leaves on this Begonia grow very large. Try it against finer foliage such as the filigree leaves of *Athyrium niponicum* var. *pictum*. **Cultivation** and **Hardiness** as for *B.* 'Comtesse de Montesquieu'.

See page 94

Begonia 'Solid Silver'

A remarkable plant with very large, puckered leaves speckled and burnished with silver. **Cultivation** and **Hardiness** as for *B.* 'Comtesse de Montesquieu'.

See page 94

Begonia fuchsioides

This is a most un-begonia-like Begonia. The upright stems bear small, toothed, glossy leaves, and the vaguely fuchsia-like flowers hang in pendulous bunches. It is a vigorous plant, and small plants can grow 16–20 in (40–50 cm) in a season, so young plants tucked in the base of a planting will become more prominent as the season progresses. **Cultivation** An easily grown plant that benefits from well-fed potting mix. **Hardiness** Frost tender.

See page 100

Bidens ferulifolia 'Golden Star'

'Golden Star' is a more compact, though still vigorous, version of the more wayward *B. ferulifolia* and is better for smaller arrangements. **Cultivation** Be prepared to cut it back if it overwhelms its neighbors. It will soon regrow. Sun. **Hardiness** This is a tender perennial, so either overwinter cuttings in a frost-free place or buy new plants in spring.

See page 70

C

Canna Orange Flower

There are many Canna hybrids available, but they are often labeled incorrectly. If you can see the flower color before you buy, so much the better. Otherwise, buy from a nursery with a good reputation. **Cultivation** Easy, fast-growing plants. Sun. **Hardiness** Protect from frost. If space is limited, the rootstock can be stored in a dark, cool but frost-free place over winter. Keep them just moist and protect from mice.

See page 100

Canna 'Pretoria'

This is also offered for sale as 'Striata', *C. malawiensis* 'Variegata', and 'Kapit'. It is a startling plant with its yellow striped leaves, but it is made all the more amazing when it opens its large, orange flowers. Unbeatable for tropical, flamboyant effect. **Cultivation** Feed and water it well to realize its full splendor. Sun. **Hardiness** Must be stored in a frost-free place over the winter.

See page 80

Canna musifolia

As a large foliage plant, there is little to beat this Canna. It grows very tall and needs a large pot. **Cultivation** Keep well-watered and feed regularly. Avoid planting it areas where the leaves can be damaged by windy weather. **Hardiness** It does not withstand freezing but can be cut back and stored in a dormant state at around 41°F (5°C).

See page 100

Calopsis paniculata

A wonderful South American Restio. The old foliage is lax and floppy, while the new is upright, giving the plant a permanently untidy look. It eventually makes a plant 6 ft (2 m) high but is worth keeping in a pot as long as possible to enjoy its feathery foliage at close quarters. **Cultivation** Needs acidic conditions. Sun. **Hardiness** Tolerates short-term cold but is best kept above freezing.

See page 92

Canna 'Black Knight'

Broad dark leaves and intense red flowers make this an ideal centerpiece for a dramatic planting. **Cultivation** Give it plenty of water and feed regularly. Removing spent flowers keeps each flower spike looking its best. Take care when watering in hard-water areas—deposits left by water splashes mark the leaves. **Hardiness** Does not tolerate freezing temperatures but can be cut back and stored in a dormant state at around 41°F (5°C).

See page 88

Canna 'Durban'

Its combination of purple leaves, pink stripes, and orange flowers must make this the most garish of the Cannas, but there is nothing better if you want a plant guaranteed to grab the attention. **Cultivation** Water well and feed regularly. Site in plenty of light but out of the wind. Sun. **Hardiness** It does not withstand freezing but can be cut back and stored in a dormant state at around 41°F (5°C).

See page 40

Carex oshimensis 'Evergold'

A reliable and cheery stalwart for winter plantings in mild regions. Its tufts of variegated, evergreen foliage go well with purple-leaved Heucheras and soft yellow winter pansies. Use it to brighten shady corners during the winter months. **Cultivation** It dislikes dry potting mix, so water regularly. **Hardiness** Zones 6–9.

See page 68

Carex comans 'Frosted Curls'

Nondescript green flowerheads borne on exceptionally long and graceful stems drape from a silvery green mound of tough, narrow foliage. It becomes a very animated plant in windy weather. **Cultivation** An easily grown plant given a moist soil and a sunny site. Occasionally comb out dead leaves with your fingers. Sun. **Hardiness** Zones 6–9.

See page 84

Carex phyllocephala "Sparkler"

Unlike most Carex, the leaves are arranged in whorls around an erect stem. It is most effective when grown in a low container where the leaves can be looked down on. **Cultivation** Keep watered and feed well. **Hardiness** Zones 7–10.

See page 68

Carex buchananii

There are several, very similar brown or "dead" grasses, and all are useful for winter and summer effect. *C. buchananii* makes a robust, upright tuft of evergreen leaves that have delightful curls at their leaf tips. **Cultivation** Dislikes waterlogged potting mix, so give good drainage. Sun. **Hardiness** With good drainage, it will survive several degrees of frost.

See page 82, 84

Carex flagellifera 'Coca-Cola'

Another "dead" grass with evergreen tufted leaves and long-stalked, brown flowerheads. Marvelous for hanging over the edge of a pot, where the long flower stalks can trail down. **Cultivation** Does not like it too dry. Sun/light shade. **Hardiness** Zones 7–9.

See page 86, 108, 112

Carex morrowii 'Fisher's Form'

The leaves of this hardy evergreen are stiff and shiny with cream stripes on a dark green background and provide valuable, year-round foliage for a shady site. **Cultivation** Water regularly, since it does not enjoy being dried out. Shade. **Hardiness** Though it stands several degrees of frost, it will benefit from the protection of a sheltered site.

See page 64

Chondropetalum mucronatum

This is a very architectural plant with the potential to grow to 5 ft (1.5 m) or more. The reedlike growth and unbranching structure give the plant a primitive character. **Cultivation** Requires a well-drained but moisture-retentive acidic potting mix. Irrigate with soft water. Full sun. **Hardiness** Tolerates several degrees of frost but may be damaged by long-term cold.

See page 92

Convolvulus cneorum

A well-behaved shrubby Convolvulus with silver, evergreen leaves and white flowers that are produced over a long period from late spring to autumn. **Cultivation** Enjoys full sun and free-draining potting mix. The drier and sunnier the situation, the more intense the leaf color. Sun. **Hardiness** Zones 8–11.

See page 42, 58, 84

Cordyline australis

Mature plants can be several yards tall, but plants between 12 in (30 cm) and 3 ft (1 m) high are suitable for container gardening. The bold, fountainlike shape makes it the ideal centerpiece for large displays. Several varieties are available, some with multicolored, striped leaves. **Cultivation** Give it full sun or light shade and a moist potting mix. **Hardiness** Tolerant of the occasional frost but likely to be damaged by persistent temperatures below freezing.

See page 36, 48

Cerinthe major 'Purpurascens'

A sophisticated-looking and fast-growing plant with flowers that unfurl from a spiral of buds. Flower and foliage colors are a perfect blend of blue-gray and purple. **Cultivation** An easy plant given good potting mix and plenty of light. Produces an abundance of easily germinated seed. Full sun. **Hardiness** Treat it as a half-hardy annual. Sow indoors in cool conditions and plant out when the danger of frost has passed.

See page 78

Ceropegia linearis subsp. *woodii*

Use its hanging stems down the outside of tall pots to emphasize the vertical line. **Cultivation** A tolerant, easily grown plant that grows quickly once established. Sun or light shade. **Hardiness** Can be left out until the first frost, after which it needs to be brought in for the winter and kept at a temperature of 46–50°F (8–10°C).

See page 110

Chlorophytum comosum 'Variegatum'

This is the Spider plant, a common houseplant but also a useful and underused foliage plant for container gardening. **Cultivation** Grow in a sheltered place to keep the leaves from being bent over by the wind. Easily propagated from the small "plantlets" that form on the end of arching shoots. Tolerates some dryness due to its water-storing tuberous roots, but keep out of scorching sun. Shade. **Hardiness** Frost tender.

See page 36

Cordyline australis 'Torbay Red'

A striking plant for giving height and shape to the middle of a planting. Its red-purple color offers plenty of scope for different color combinations. **Cultivation** Give it full sun or light shade and a moist potting mix. **Hardiness** Tolerant of the occasional frost but likely to be damaged by persistent temperatures below freezing.

See page 66

Cordyline australis Purpurea Group

This name covers a range of plants with purple leaves of different shades. Shop around and select the deepest color you can find. **Cultivation** Give it full sun or light shade and moist potting mix. **Hardiness** Tolerant of the occasional frost but likely to be damaged by persistent temperatures below freezing.

See page 28, 80

Crocosmia 'Star of the East'

Crocosmias are valuable for their foliage as well as their bright flowers. They come in colors from pale yellow to fiery red and in heights ranging from 16 in (40 cm) to over 3 ft (1 m). All are good plants for late-summer color. **Cultivation** Dormant corms can be planted in autumn among a hardy planting, or use young divisions in spring among tender plants. Full sun and moist potting mix. Sun. **Hardiness** Zones 6–9.

See page 100, 108

Cuphea 'Tiny Mice'

Flowers of an intense color with vaguely mouselike faces give this shrubby plant plenty of character. Its bushy habit and dark green leaves make it a good filler for the base of a display. **Cultivation** An easily-grown plant for full sun. Pinch out the shoot tips to encourage bushy growth. Sun. **Hardiness** A tender perennial that can be overwintered at around 50°F (10°C).

See page 80

Cuphea hyssopifolia 'Alba'

Tiny white flowers and small leaves give this bushy little plant a busy, frothy look. Ideal for filling in around taller plants and for giving newly planted displays a fuller look. Pink and purple varieties are available. **Cultivation** An easy, trouble-free plant requiring no special conditions. Sun or shade. **Hardiness** A frost-tender perennial that needs a minimum winter temperature of at least 45°F (7°C).

See page 36

Cuphea ignea

A bushy evergreen shrub producing its tubular orange flowers in good numbers and over a long period. It provides interesting detail within a planting and is a good filler around more upright plants. **Cultivation** Pinch out shoot tips when young to encourage bushy growth. Easily propagated from seed or by cuttings taken in late summer. Sun. **Hardiness** Requires a minimum winter temperature of around 43°F (6°C).

See page 108

Dahlia 'Ragged Robin'

Deeply cut, almost feathery foliage and small flowers with uneven petals give it a romantic and natural quality that is absent in the traditional large-flowered Dahlias. **Cultivation** Water well and feed regularly. Full sun or light shade. **Hardiness** Frost tender. Wait until the foliage is blackened by frost, then cut back the stems. Lift and store the tubers in a frost-free environment away from hungry mice.

See page 88

Dahlia 'Roxy'

Many Dahlias are too tall to be useful container plants, but this short variety—with magenta flowers and almost black leaves— only grows to about 16 in (40 cm). **Cultivation** Water well and feed regularly. Full sun or light shade. **Hardiness** Frost tender. Wait until the foliage is blackened by frost before cutting back the stems. Lift and store the tubers in a frost-free environment away from hungry mice.

See page 30

Dichondra 'Silver Falls'

A very good plant for providing dense, trailing foliage. **Cultivation** Easily grown. Stems root readily if tucked into the potting mix, giving rise to more shoots and even denser growth. It is slow to start but once it is established and the temperature warms up, it grows vigorously. Full sun. **Hardiness** A tender perennial that is likely to survive the first few light frosts, but needs to be kept at a minimum winter temperature of 45°F (7°C).

See page 72, 74

Cussonia paniculata

Mature plants reach 12–15 ft (4–5 m), but younger specimens are ideal for architectural container displays. Few plants come near it for impressive foliage. **Cultivation** Ensure good drainage. Tolerant of occasional drying out. Sun. **Hardiness** Tolerates occasional frost, but for guaranteed health, keep at a minimum of 45°F (7°C) during the winter.

See page 72

D

Dahlia 'Bednall Beauty'

Its wonderful combination of glossy, dark, divided foliage and crimson flowers makes this worthy of a pot on its own. At around 20 in (50 cm) tall, it is one of the shorter dahlias. **Cultivation** Water well and feed regularly. Full sun or light shade. **Hardiness** Frost tender. Wait until the foliage is blackened by the frost, then cut back the stems. Lift and store the tubers in a frost-free environment away from hungry mice.

See page 112

E

Echeveria glauca

An important foliage plant. Try it in color combinations with white, black, pink, and purple. The multicolored flowers are fun, but if they upset your color theme, cut them off. **Cultivation** An easy succulent that, given moist potting mix, will grow into large rosettes by the end of the season. Sun and light shade. **Hardiness** Frost tender. Overwinter at a minimum of 45°F (7°C).

See page 56

Elymus magellanicus

A well-behaved, clump-forming perennial grass with pale blue leaves. It can look scruffy, so tidy up any dead leaves before planting and then periodically during the season. **Cultivation** Provide well-drained potting mix and plenty of light. Sun. **Hardiness** Zones 6–9; needs good winter drainage to prevent the plant from rotting.

See page 74

Eucomis bicolor

An impressive flowering bulb that can be used in permanent plantings for its broad, strappy foliage, big flower spikes, and large seedheads. Plants emptied out of pots at the end of the season can be planted in the garden. **Cultivation** Easily grown in fertile potting mix. Sun. **Hardiness** Surprisingly hardy for such an exotic-looking flower. With good drainage and deep planting, it will survive to 14°F (−10°C).

See page 48

Euonymus fortunei 'Emerald 'n' Gold'

A reliable, if a little predictable, evergreen shrub. It is a tough plant that, given reasonable care, will thrive for many years in a pot as the mainstay of a permanent planting. The leaves take on reddish tints during the winter, particularly if the plant is undernourished. **Cultivation** Trim to shape as and when needed. Feed regularly, particularly in permanent plantings. **Hardiness** Zones 5–9.

See page 38

Hakonechloa macra

Though not as popular as its variegated form, the plain green species has a softness and grace not found in other forms. The wispy seedheads add to its charm. **Cultivation** Grow in cool conditions and keep moist. Sun/shade. **Hardiness** Zones 5–9.

See page 68

Hakonechloa macra 'Aureola'

A low-growing grass whose bright yellow, variegated leaves can be used to enliven a planting. As they mature, the leaves arch over, forming a soft mound that is ideal as an underplanting to larger plants. **Cultivation** Keep the potting mix moist and feed well. Keep out of scorching sun to prevent the leaves from being bleached. **Hardiness** Zones 5–9.

See page 50

Fatsia japonica

Marvelous shiny foliage and a robust shape combine to make this a very good center-piece for a planting. The broad leaves are a perfect foil for feathery or spiky textures. **Cultivation** Grow in a shady site out of strong winds, and feed and water regularly to keep the leaves in good condition. Shade. **Hardiness** Withstands several degrees of frost but may be damaged by persistent freezing temperatures.

See page 114

G

Geranium 'Ann Folkard'

A vigorous perennial with trailing stems that will either tumble out of a pot or scramble their way up through the planting. Younger leaves are yellow-green, turning green as they age. **Cultivation** Once established in the pot, it grows rapidly, and some of the shoots will have to be snipped off or redirected if they are not to overwhelm the rest of the plants. **Hardiness** Zones 5–9.

See page 104

Hebe pimeliodes 'Quicksilver'

A plant with tiny gray leaves and wiry black stems, this is unlikely to make you stand back in awe, but when used as an element of detail to build an overall richness to a planting, it can be very effective. **Cultivation** The leaf color is intensified by dry conditions. Full sun. **Hardiness** Zones 8–10.

See page 74

Hedera helix 'Amber Waves'

This reliable and easy-to-grow evergreen develops dense trailing foliage that creeps over the rim of a pot, softening its edge. It provides good year-round color in mild regions. **Cultivation** Though tolerant of neglect, a good, rich potting mix and regular feeding and watering produce a much healthier plant with better color and therefore more impact. Sun or shade. **Hardiness** Zones 5–11.

See page 90

Hedera helix 'Lalla Rookh'

A versatile plant that can be encouraged to climb, to trail, or to grow flat across the top of the pot to provide an ornamental finish to the potting-mix surface. **Cultivation** Water and feed regularly. Hederas are tolerant plants, so prune, train, and pinch out stems whenever there is a need. **Hardiness** Zones 5–11.

See page 90

Helichrysum italicum

An evergreen shrub with narrow, curry-scented leaves. Good for year-round effect in mild areas. **Cultivation** Enjoys hot and dry conditions. Poor soil will result in a more intense silver color. To keep its size in check, cut back any time between spring and late summer. **Hardiness** Likely to be damaged at temperatures below 23°F (–6°C). More tolerant of cold if the potting mix is kept on the dry side.

See page 58

Helichrysum petiolare

This is an essential trailing container plant that can be used in many situations. It flows over the edge of a pot with style, and its neat, felted leaves are a foil for a wide variety of colors and textures. **Cultivation** A vigorous tender perennial that enjoys regular feeding. Cut out unwanted or misplaced shoots when required. **Hardiness** To overwinter successfully, it needs 45°F (7°C) minimum. It is best bought new each spring.

See page 44, 110

Helichrysum petiolare 'Limelight'

This is one of my top five container plants. **Cultivation** It needs to be well fed and watered to look its best. Hot, scorching sun will bleach and distort the leaves, so keep it in light shade to get the best from the foliage. **Hardiness** Overwintered plants often look scruffy, and young plants grow quickly, so it is better to buy new plants each year.

See page 44, 66

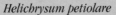

I

Impatiens 'Accent Cranberry'

Most Impatiens have harsh colors that are difficult to place in a display. 'Cranberry' is a far easier plant to use and ideal for richly colored displays. **Cultivation** Tolerates sun if kept well watered, but prefers a shady site or the shade from surrounding plants. Sun/shade. **Hardiness** Frost-tender perennial that can be overwintered as a houseplant; otherwise, buy each year.

See page 88

Impatiens 'Accent White'

Except for the snowdrop, no plant has such a pure crystalline white flower. The perfect combination of its flower color and rich green leaves puts this in my top five container plants. **Cultivation** Tolerates hot sun if kept well watered, but prefers a shady site or the shade from surrounding plants. Sun/shade. **Hardiness** Frost-tender perennial that can be overwintered as a houseplant or bought new each year.

See page 36

Heuchera 'Can-Can'

Dark purple foliage is useful for giving visual weight to the base of a planting. 'Can-Can' is ideal for this task, especially in hardy, year-round plantings. **Cultivation** Feed and water regularly and keep out of cold winter winds. It may be damaged by vine weevils. Sun or shade. **Hardiness** Zones 4–8.

See page 34

Heuchera 'Plum Pudding'

'Plum Pudding' holds up well against winter weather and is one of the best Heucheras for winter effect. **Cultivation** Feed and water regularly and keep out of cold winter winds. May be damaged by vine weevils. Sun or shade. **Hardiness** Zones 4–8.

See page 96

Heuchera 'Silver Scrolls'

Heucheras are among the best foliage plants for hardy container gardening. 'Silver Scrolls' is just one of many dark or marbled-leaf varieties. All are worth trying. Their persistent flower stalks can add useful vertical height to a planting. **Cultivation** Keep out of drying winds and do not let the potting mix dry out. May be damaged by vine weevils. Sun or shade. **Hardiness** Zones 4–8.

See page 84

Imperata cylindrica 'Rubra'

A stunning perennial grass with green leaves that quickly mature to deep red. **Cultivation** This plant enjoys rich potting mix, so incorporate plenty of organic matter and feed and water well. **Hardiness** Zones 5–9; does better with frost protection and just-moist soil.

See page 88

Ipomoea batatas 'Blackie'

Another of my top five plants. Use this small, compact plant on its own for its wonderful combination of foliage, shape, and color, or mix it into small-scale displays. It does not climb. **Cultivation** Keep moist and well-fed. Propagate from cuttings. Sun or shade. **Hardiness** Provide a winter temperature of at least 45–46°F (7–8°C).

See page 32, 94

Isoplexis canariensis

The way this plant presents its color on upright flower spikes is useful to the container gardener. Trained as a standard, it gives instant height to a display, but it is equally good as low, leafy plant at the base of a planting. **Cultivation** An easily grown plant, given an open sunny site and a well-fed potting mix. Sun. **Hardiness** A tender perennial needing a minimum winter temperature of 41°F (5°C).

See page 100

Isotoma (Laurentia) axillaris

A pretty plant with a gentle nature, useful as a fluffy filler among stronger plants or to create a romantic mood with pinks and whites. **Cultivation** An annual that succeeds in any reasonable potting mix that is not kept too wet. Sun. **Hardiness** This a tender annual that should not be put out until the risk of frost has passed.

See page 52

Juncus effusus f. spiralis

A tangle of a plant with glossy, cylindrical stems twisted and curled in any number of ways. Good for year-round effect. **Cultivation** Its natural habitat is one of moist or even wet acidic soil, so regular watering and a neutral to acidic potting mix are important. Snip out old brown stems with scissors to prevent the plant from looking scruffy. **Hardiness** Zones 6–9.

See page 34

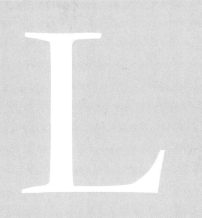

Lamium galeobdolon 'Hermann's Pride'

A spreading perennial with silver-netted foliage and hooded yellow flowers on erect stems. **Cultivation** Given moist potting mix, it makes a dense vigorous mat of foliage. The flowers can be left or cut off, depending on your color theme. Shade. **Hardiness** Zones 4–8.

See page 68

Lavandula 'Fathead'

Their tolerance of dry conditions makes Lavenders good container plants. This is a fairly compact plant with dumpy, almost round flowerheads, but there are dozens of different-sized and colored varieties available. **Cultivation** Provide a sunny site and well-drained potting mix. Cut off flower stalks after flowering. To keep in shape, trim back into previous season's growth, but not into old wood, in spring. **Hardiness** Zones 8–9.

See page 28

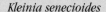

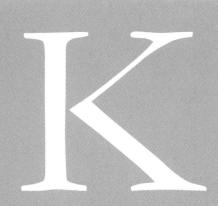

K

Kalanchoe tomentosa

A textural delight. Useful for thoughtful plantings where tactile surfaces and shape are important. **Cultivation** Tolerates dry conditions, but will grow more quickly with regular summer watering. **Hardiness** A tender succulent that requires minimum winter temperatures of 50–54°F (10–12°C) and plenty of light.

See page 72

Kleinia senecioides

Another of my top five plants. It has glaucous, fleshy fingers on a vigorous trailing plant that can reach 28 in (70 cm) or more in a season. **Cultivation** Despite its drought-tolerant look, water it regularly and it will respond by growing rapidly. **Hardiness** A frost-tender perennial needing a winter temperature of at least 50°F (10°C) and plenty of light.

See page 74, 112

Leymus arenarius

A dramatic perennial plant with coarse, powder blue, grassy leaves. Its invasive nature can be a nuisance, but given a pot to itself, its distinctive style can be used to advantage where a clean and sharp effect is needed. Cut off the unattractive seedheads. **Cultivation** Very tolerant of hot, dry conditions and poor soil and does not enjoy wet potting mix. Sun. **Hardiness** Zones 4–10.

See page 42, 110

Liriope muscari 'Variegata'

This evergreen perennial has a much brighter creamy yellow variegation than this picture shows and is a very showy plant. Good for shady conditions. An added bonus is the dense, upright heads of small mauve flowers that are produced in late summer and autumn. **Cultivation** Dislikes wet potting mix and tolerates dryness surprisingly well for such a lush-looking plant. Shade. **Hardiness** Zones 5–10.

See page 68

Lotus hirsutus

This is in my top ten plants for its soft foliage and pink-tinged white flowers. They make it an effective foil for a wide range of colors and textures. **Cultivation** Best grown quite hard to keep it compact, because too rich a potting mix causes straggly growth and less intense leaf color. Sun. **Hardiness** Hardy to 14°F (–10°C) or lower in free-draining, dry conditions.

See page 62

Lotus maculatus

A tender, perennial, trailing plant valuable for both its orange flowers and its feathery leaves. Young plants can grow 24 in (60 cm) or more by the end of the season. **Cultivation** An early summer flowering is usually followed by a reduced display before a late summer flourish. For the best display, do not let this plant dry out. Feed well. Sun. **Hardiness** Provide a minimum winter temperature of 41°F (5°C).

See page 86

M

Melianthus major

This plant is right at the top of my list of all-time greats for large containers. It has very dramatic large leaves that get grayer as they mature and have an interesting peanut-butter smell. **Cultivation** Responds well to feeding. Prone to whitefly in the greenhouse. Give it plenty of space. Sun. **Hardiness** Tolerates a few degrees of frost but is best kept above 41°F (5°C) for the winter.

See page 110

O

Ophiopogon planiscapus 'Nigrescens'

Invaluable hardy perennial for small displays of both tender and hardy plants. There is nothing blacker. Perfect with grays and whites. **Cultivation** Easy to grow in a pot or start in the garden for container use. Splits readily into small tufts for tucking into your display. Sun or shade. **Hardiness** Zones 6–11.

See page 32, 56, 84

Opuntia lindheimeri

Because of their adaptations to extreme environments, succulents are some of the most structural and elemental plants available. Not easy to use in combinations, they are often best displayed as individual specimens. **Cultivation** Use a free-draining. soil-based potting mix and water regularly during the summer. Sun. **Hardiness** Withstands several degrees of frost, provided it has very free drainage.

See page 76

Mimulus aurantiacus

An open and lax shrub with shiny, sticky leaves. Few other plants can offer the same soft coloring. Darker and paler varieties are available, and all are good plants. **Cultivation** Overwinter in a dry atmosphere to discourage rotting. Pinch out the growing tips to encourage a more bushy habit. Sun. **Hardiness** Provide a winter temperature of 48–50°F (8°–10°C).

See page 86

N

Nicotiana 'Lime Green'

There are many colors of annual bedding Nicotianas, but few as distinctive as this. Bear in mind that it grows to 20–24 in (50–60 cm) when planting young plants into a display. All are easy plants to grow. **Cultivation** Raise from seeds sown in spring or buy young plants. Deadhead regularly to encourage more flowers. Sun or light shade. **Hardiness** Plant out after all danger of frost has passed.

See page 48

Osteospermum jucundum

A vigorous spreading plant the produces flowers nonstop from late spring until the first frosts of winter. Its low mats of gray-tinted, evergreen foliage make this a good plant for permanent planting. **Cultivation** Feed and water regularly. Make sure the pot drains freely if using in a year-round planting. Sun. **Hardiness** Possibly the toughest of all the Osteospermums. With good drainage, it withstands temperatures as low as 14°F (–10°C).

See page 66, 96

Osteospermum 'Serena'

There is a wide range of Osteospermums now available, including pinks, purples, yellows, and white. All are good floriferous plants, and the newer compact varieties are particularly good for small arrangements. I particularly like the subtlety of this variety's fragile, pink-brown color. **Cultivation** Deadhead for continuous flowering. Sun or light shade. **Hardiness** Protect from frost.

See page 82, 86

Pelargonium 'Bushfire'

This is a regal Pelargonium of moderately upright growth. Regal Pelargoniums generally have fewer larger flowers and tougher toothed leaves than the more common zonal pelargoniums. **Cultivation** Deadhead regularly to prevent spent petals from falling onto the leaves and causing rot. Sun. **Hardiness** Provide a minimum winter temperature of 46–50°F (8 and 10°C).

See page 60

Pelargonium 'Harvard'

The trailing or ivy-leaf Pelargoniums are substantial foliage plants as well as having good flowers. 'Harvard' has rich, regal red flowers and can grow 24 in (60 cm) or more by the end of the season. **Cultivation** Feed and water regularly. Deadhead as each truss of flowers fades. **Hardiness** Provide a minimum winter temperature of 39°F (4°C).

See page 30

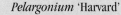

Pelargonium tomentosum

Velvety leaves that smell like peppermint when rubbed make this one of my favorite foliage plants. It is vigorous and can put on 28 in (70 cm) or more of spreading growth in a season. Flowers are small and insignificant. Good in large containers, or on its own spilling out of a low flat planter. **Cultivation** Easily grown. Sun or light shade. **Hardiness** Provide a minimum winter temperature of 39°F (4°C).

See page 100

Penstemon 'Blackbird'

There are many varieties of hybrid Penstemons; all are floriferous and all make good container plants. Colors range from purple to pink and white. 'Blackbird' is one of the darkest. Though usually reliable, it flowered poorly in my container display. **Cultivation** Cut out spent flower stems to promote new flowering shoots. For protection, do not remove topgrowth until after the winter. **Hardiness** Zones 7–10; does best if well-drained.

See page 104

Persicaria microcephala

A leafy perennial with a spreading habit, growing to 12 in (30 cm) or so in height. A good filler around more floriferous plants. **Cultivation** Enjoys moist potting mix and a situation out of scorching midday sun. Sun/half-shade. **Hardiness** Zones 5–9.

See page 82

Pelargonium Ignescens

It is worth looking beyond the usual regal and zonal Pelargoniums and discovering the rest of the species and their close hybrids. There is a diverse range of leaf shapes and flower colors. *P.* 'Ignescens' is a primary hybrid with an upright, open habit and flowers of intense fiery red. **Cultivation** Water, feed, and deadhead regularly. Sun. **Hardiness** Provide a minimum winter temperature of 39°F (4°C).

See page 60

Pelargonium 'Lady Plymouth'

Another top ten plant. Unbeatable variegated foliage on a robust, easily satisfied, leafy and compact plant—what more could you ask for? Scent? Then you have it. Rub the leaves for a spicy eucalyptus smell. The pink flowers are small and should be ignored or removed. **Cultivation** Water, feed, and deadhead regularly. Sun or shade. **Hardiness** Provide a minimum winter temperature of 39°F (4°C).

See page 98, 114

Pelargonium 'Sassy Dark Red'

I like this plant for its, compact habit, its propensity to flower, and its intensity of color. Fully saturated colors like this cannot help but catch the eye. **Cultivation** Water, feed, and deadhead regularly. Sun. **Hardiness** Provide a minimum winter temperature of 39°F (4°C).

See page 60

Persicaria microcephala 'Red Dragon'

A superb foliage plant despite its vigorous growth. In large pots, it finds its way through other plants, sending out shoots in unexpected places. Makes an attractive specimen in a pot on its own. **Cultivation** An herbaceous perennial that needs moist potting mix and regular feeding. In poor conditions, the leaves turn brown and lose their luster. Cut back wayward shoots at any time. Sun/shade. **Hardiness** Zones 5–9.

See page 30

Petasites japonicus 'Nishiki-buki'

This is a very imposing garden thug. Well-fed plants produce leaves up to 24 in (60 cm) across. Its spreading shoots are unstoppable in the garden. Containing it in a pot is the only way to enjoy it in a small garden. **Cultivation** Give it plenty of water and feed well to realize its full glory. Tolerates sun but soon wilts in a small pot. Sun/Shade. **Hardiness** Zones 5–9.

See page 102

Petunia 'Blue Trailing'

Good blue-flowered container plants are rare and should be cherished. This blue Petunia has a good balance of flower and foliage that prevents it from dominating the planting. **Cultivation** Regular deadheading ensures continuity of flowering and keeps the plant neat. Sun. **Hardiness** Treat as an annual. Do not plant out if there is any danger of frost, and discard at the end of the season.

See page 62

Petunia 'Million Bells' Red

Petunias and their close relatives come in all sizes. These small-flowered Petunias have considerably more charm than their larger counterparts and are easier to use in smaller, more intimate arrangements. **Cultivation** They do not enjoy wet potting mix, so be careful not to overwater. Sun. **Hardiness** Treat as an annual. Do not plant out if there is any danger of frost, and discard at the end of the season.

See page 50

Petunia 'Million Bells' Cherry

A rich color on a small attractive plant. Ideal for squeezing in among leafy plants to add highlights of color. **Cultivation** Slightly prone to rotting at the beginning of the season if kept too wet and cold. Dead-heading is a beneficial though rather fiddly job. Sun. **Hardiness** Treat as an annual. Do not plant out if there is any danger of frost, and discard at the end of the season.

See page 50

Petunia 'Prism Sunshine'

A flower for soft effect. Plant breeders have developed large-flowered Petunias that are much more resistant to wind and rain than they used to be, and this type has proved particularly reliable for me. **Cultivation** As with all Petunias, regular deadheading is beneficial. Sun/light shade. **Hardiness** Treat as an annual. Do not plant out if there is any danger of frost, and discard at the end of the season.

See page 54, 70

Phormium hybrid

There is an ever-growing range of variegated hybrid Phormiums. Colors range from almost black to pink and bright yellow. The combination of colors and strong architectural qualities makes them very valuable to the container gardener. **Cultivation** Give them a free-draining potting mix, but water well in the summer. Sun/light shade. **Hardiness** With good drainage and a sheltered position, they are likely to tolerate temperatures as low as 23°F (–5°C).

See page 40

Phormium tenax

This is one of the most imposing plants to use as the centerpiece of an arrangement. It is potentially a very large plant, but in a container, its growth rate is controlled and it can be kept small enough for many years. **Cultivation** Its tall evergreen leaves act like sails, so beware of siting it in exposed positions. Sun/light shade. **Hardiness** Tolerates 23°F (–5°C) or lower if kept dry and protected from cold winds.

See page 84

Phormium tenax 'Variegatum'

A striking evergreen plant with stiffly erect leaves. Ideal for structural, year-round arrangements. **Cultivation** Give it a sunny position. Use free-draining potting mix and water well in summer. Sun. **Hardiness** With good drainage and a sheltered position, it is likely to tolerate –5°C (23°F) or even less°.

See page 68

Petunia 'Trailing Red'

I chose this Petunia for its intense color. It is always better to buy your plants in flower so you know exactly what color you are getting. Labels can be misleading. **Cultivation** Regular deadheading ensures continuity of flowering and also keeps the plant neat. Sun. **Hardiness** Treat as an annual. Do not plant out if there is any danger of frost, and discard at the end of the season.

See page 38

Petunia 'Trailing White'

Trailing Petunias and their relatives the Surfinias are prolific plants and valuable providers of bold blocks of color. But be careful not to let their mass of flowers overwhelm the planting. Be prepared to cut out whole stems to maintain balance in the display. **Cultivation** Deadhead regularly. Sun/light shade. **Hardiness** Treat as an annual. Do not plant out if there is any danger of frost, and discard at the end of the season.

See page 44

Petunia 'White'

This is near the top of my list of flowers for cool and romantic effect. The purity of its whiteness stands out. **Cultivation** Keep it out of areas that are exposed to strong winds. Control slugs and snails, which enjoy eating the flowers. Sun/light shade. **Hardiness** Treat as an annual. Do not plant out if there is any danger of frost, and discard at the end of the growing season.

See page 54

Plectranthus argentatus

A textural delight. Its neutral color works well with all kinds of other colors. Its soft lilac flowers are held in open heads. Evergreen. **Cultivation** Give it plenty of light but avoid windy sites. The stems are likely to snap as the plant gets bigger. Pinching out the shoot tips at regular intervals encourages bushy growth and a compact plant. Sun. **Hardiness** Needs a winter temperature between 46° and 50°F (8–10°C).

See page 74

Plectranthus ciliatus

This plant has never flowered for me, but that does not diminish its value as an evergreen foliage plant. It has a trailing habit and can grow 24 in (60 cm) or more in a season. Its effect is dark, but that makes it an ideal foil for whites and silvers. **Cultivation** Keep it watered and well-fed, and out of scorching sunshine. Sun/shade. **Hardiness** Give it a winter minimum temperature of around 46°F (8°C).

See page 74

Plectranthus madagascariensis 'Variegated Mintleaf'

Often labeled as Plectranthus Variegated, this is an easier plant than the more traditional "trailing nepeta" (*Glechoma hederacea* 'Variegata'), which always suffers from mildew in my plantings. The fleshy leaves are more substantial, the arching stems more elegant, and the crisp variegation gives the whole plant more sparkle. **Cultivation** An easy and trouble-free plant. Sun/shade. **Hardiness** Overwinter at around 46°F (8°C).

See page 36, 98

Plectranthus zatarhendii

This is a low-growing, pot-hugging, identical twin of *Plectranthus argentatus* (*see p179*). The vigorous trailing stems put on over 24 in (60 cm) of growth if well cared-for. **Cultivation** An undemanding plant. The trailing stems will root when in contact with the soil and can be a useful and easy source of new plants. Sun. **Hardiness** Overwinter at around 46°F (8°C).

See page 78

R

Rhodochiton atrosanguineus

A tender perennial climber with distinctive hanging flowers. **Cultivation** Raised from spring-sown seed, it grows rapidly and makes a sizable plant by early summer. Do not put plants outdoors until the danger of frost has passed. Provide twiggy support. Prone to attack by whitefly in a greenhouse. Sun. **Hardiness** Provide a minimum winter temperature of 46°F (8°C).

See page 30, 78

Salvia splendens 'Purple'

A useful alternative to the usual bright red, dirty white, or weak pink varieties. The stumpy growth is not elegant, but it provides solid color. **Cultivation** Raise from spring-sown seed or buy young plants. Sun. **Hardiness** Treat as an annual and discard at the end of the season.

See page 46

Sambucus nigra 'Black Lace'

A hardy deciduous shrub that is unremarkable in the winter, but in summer its deeply cut purple foliage is extremely useful for a wispy effect. **Cultivation** At the end of the season, remove the plant from its display and pot it into as small a pot as is practical. Prune it back to approximately 12 in (30 cm). Overwinter it outdoors, then plant it into a new display in spring. Sun/shade. **Hardiness** Zones 4–7.

See page 30, 38

Senecio macroglossus 'Variegatus'

Here is another houseplant ideal for outdoor ornamental use. Given the benefit of a large container and the warmth of summer, its growth outdoors is rapid. **Cultivation** Do not plant out until the risk of frost has passed. Provide support for the twining stems. Sun/shade. **Hardiness** Minimum winter temperature of 45°F (7°C).

See page 54

S

See page 112

Salvia 'Raspberry Royale'

An open, twiggy, semievergreen shrub. The branches are brittle, so handle with care. **Cultivation** To reuse this shrub, dig it out of its display at the end of the season and pot it. It tolerates a few degrees of frost, but it is safer to keep it frost-free during the winter. In spring, cut back the branches to about 8 in (20 cm) before planting into a new display. Sun. **Hardiness** Zones 9–11.

See page 112

Salvia farinacea 'Victoria'

Valuable for its bushy foliage, the rich color of its flowers, and its upright shape. **Cultivation** Although this is a tender herbaceous perennial, it is better treated as an annual. Raise new plants from seed sown in late winter or spring or buy young plants in early summer. Sun. **Hardiness** Do not plant out until the danger of frost has passed. It continues to flower until the first hard frost.

See page 104

Senecio petasitis

A large, velvet-leaved plant that produces big heads of small yellow flowers on mature plants. It needs to be touched for the full sensory experience. **Cultivation** Removing the growing tips when young encourages branching and suckering from the roots. **Hardiness** Withstands the first few frosts but ideally should be kept frost-free during the winter.

See page 98

Silene uniflora 'Swan Lake'

A tough plant whose small blue leaves and long flower stems give elegance to the double pompon flowers. **Cultivation** Requires sunshine and good drainage. This plant grows in seaside conditions, so it tolerates wind, sun and dryness, but it becomes a far better plant if treated more generously. It dislikes winter waterlogging. Sun. **Hardiness** Zones 4–7.

See page 42

Solanum rantonnetii

An ornamental, evergreen shrubby member of the potato family. **Cultivation** Trained as a standard in the container portrait (*see page 52*), it works equally well as a small shrub, although it needs a large pot. Regularly pinching out the growing tips keeps it compact and ensures plenty of new shoots and an abundance of flowers. Feed and water regularly. Sun. **Hardiness** Overwinter at a temperature of at least 45°F (7°C).

See page 52

Solenostemon 'Midnight'

Leaves of Solenostemon (Coleus) varieties range from whole to so deeply lobed and twisted as to appear shredded. 'Midnight' is as scallop-edged as I like to go. **Cultivation** If kept moist, it will tolerate full sun. Large plants tend to snap in very windy conditions. Cuttings root easily—putting them in a glass of water on a windowsill works perfectly well. Sun/shade. **Hardiness** Provide a winter minimum of 45°F (7°C).

See page 38

Solenostemon 'Black Prince'

Single-colored varieties are the easiest to work with. The matt finish on the leaves makes this variety especially effective in container displays. **Cultivation** The flowers of the Solenostemon are rather small and ineffective. They are best pinched out as they form. Sun/shade. **Hardiness** Provide a winter minimum of 45°F (7°C).

See page 62

Solenostemon hybrid

There are hundreds of named varieties of what are more commonly known as Coleus. Yet more unnamed hybrid seedlings are offered as mixed selections in garden centers. **Cultivation** Keep well-watered and feed regularly. Keep out of exposed sites because blustery winds can snap off the branches of larger plants. Pinch out flower buds. Sun/shade. **Hardiness** Provide a winter minimum temperature of 45°F (7°C).

See page 82

T

Tellima grandiflora 'Forest Frost'

An evergreen perennial with open spikes of green and pink flowers in late spring. The foliage takes on reddish tints in winter. **Cultivation** Cut out the flower stems as soon as they fade, or sooner if they ruin the look of your display. Though tolerant of dry conditions, a better plant will result from regular watering and occasional feeding through the summer. Shade. **Hardiness** Zones 5–8.

See page 64

Teucrium scorodonia 'Crispum'

An interesting evergreen subshrub with crinkly-textured leaves. Ideal for hardy textural mixes. Its green flowers only add to its overall effect. **Cultivation** This is an easily satisfied plant, tolerant of shade and dry conditions; however, a much fresher-looking plant will be produced by regular watering and feeding. **Hardiness** Zones 6–9.

See page 34

Solenostemon 'Juliet Quartermain'

Solenostemons provide some of the richest foliage color, but they need good light to be at their best. Look out for named varieties, such as this one, that have been selected for their reliability and color. **Cultivation** Keep well-watered and feed regularly. Keep out of exposed sites because wind can snap off the branches of larger plants. Pinch out growing tips to encourage bushiness. Take off flower buds. Sun/shade. **Hardiness** Provide a winter minimum temperature of 45°F (7°C).

See page 106

Solenostemon 'Winter Sun'

Well-grown specimens of Solenostemon, particularly the single-colored varieties, have sufficient character to stand alone as specimens. They are quick-growing given plenty of light and rich potting mix. **Cultivation** To produce high-quality plants, feed weekly with a balanced plant food and make sure the plant does not dry out. Keep out of buffeting winds and pinch out young flower buds. Sun/shade. **Hardiness** Provide a winter minimum of 45°F (7°C).

See page 40

Sphaeralcea 'Newleaze Coral'

A sun-loving, open, and upright subshrub. The mallowlike flowers are produced from early summer until the first frosts. **Cultivation** Needs well-drained potting mix and a sunny position. **Hardiness** With good drainage and a sheltered position, it withstands several degrees of frost, but it needs frost protection to be totally safe.

See page 60

Thunbergia alata

This cheerful climbing plant is very useful for background height in a container. Given a long growing season, it may reach over 5 ft (1.5 m). In shorter arrangements, wrap the stems back on each other. **Cultivation** This is a tender perennial plant that is usually treated as an annual. Raise from seed sown indoors in spring. It dislikes cold, so plant out after all danger of frost has passed. Sun. **Hardiness** Overwinter at 45°F (7°C) minimum.

See page 54, 108

Tibouchina urvilleana

One of the top plants for a flamboyant effect, on account of its large, exotic-colored flowers. The foliage is covered in soft down. **Cultivation** It can make a large shrub with a framework of sturdy branches and is ideal as a single specimen, but it is also tolerant of being cut back each spring to bring it down to manageable proportions for a mixed display. Sun. **Hardiness** Provide a winter minimum of 43°F (5°C).

See page 104

Tolmiea menziesii 'Taff's Gold'

A leafy perennial valuable for its shade-tolerant foliage, which makes a luxuriant clump when well-fed and watered. The early-season flower spikes have little impact as a design feature but reveal a complex mix of brown, pink, purple, orange, and green filamentous flowers when studied close up. **Cultivation** An easily satisfied plant given moisture, shade, and a rich potting mix. Shade. **Hardiness** Zones 6–9.

See page 102

Tradescantia pallida 'Purpurea'

A popular houseplant but rarely used outdoors, which is a shame, because it is an extremely useful foliage plant for container gardening. **Cultivation** The foliage has a bloom that is easily rubbed off, so handle with care. Splashes of hard water also dry to leave disfiguring marks. Sun/shade. **Hardiness** Tolerates the first frosts, but then needs to be kept at a winter temperature of around 50°F (10°C).

See page 94

Uncinia rubra

A richly colored evergreen grass that is lovely when young but becomes straggly after a few seasons, so use young plants for best effect. **Cultivation** Grow in a fertile, free-draining potting mix, but keep moist in the summer. Sun. **Hardiness** Tolerates several degrees of frost when grown in well-drained conditions.

See page 80

Verbena Tapien Violet

There are many seed strains of Verbena. Some are trailing plants; others are erect and bushy. I chose this Verbena for its rich color and trailing habit. To be sure you get the color you require, buy your plants in flower. **Cultivation** Deadheading is important for successive flowering. Sun. Prone to attack by aphids. **Hardiness** Grow as an annual. Plant out after the last frost and discard at the end of the season.

See page 44, 46

Vinca minor 'Illumination'

A variegated variety of the common Periwinkle. Its evergreen quality makes it ideal for year-round displays. Slower-growing than its all-green counterpart, its stems still grow up to 16–20 in (40–50 cm) long in a season. With me, it does not produce many flowers. They are blue and can either be left on or pinched off if they upset your color theme. **Cultivation** A tough plant and easy to care for. Sun. **Hardiness** Zones 4–9.

See page 50

Viola 'Apricot'

Violas are good for providing bold patches of color, particularly during the colder months when nothing else is flowering. The summer varieties, like 'Apricot', give a relaxed, cottage feel to a planting. Avoid mixed colors if you want a unified and designed look. **Cultivation** Look out for damage by aphids. Sun. **Hardiness** A tough plant that will withstand freezing temperatures but is best discarded at the end of the summer.

See page 86

V

Verbena 'Aztec Red Trailing'

It was the intensity of its color that attracted me to this vigorous trailing variety. Few other plants offer such a pure red. **Cultivation** Deadheading is important for successive flowering. Keep well fed and watered. Plants under drought stress are susceptible to mildew. Aphids can be a problem, so check regularly. Sun. **Hardiness** Grow as an annual. Plant out after the last frost and discard at the end of the season.

See page 38

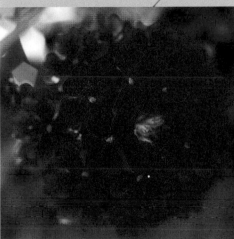

Verbena 'Diamond Merci'

This is a vigorous trailing variety with good disease resistance and a rich burgundy color that is unusual among Verbenas. **Cultivation** Deadheading is important for successive flowering. Prone to attack by aphids. Benefits from regular feeding. Sun. **Hardiness** Grow as an annual. Plant out after the last frost and discard at the end of the season.

See page 46

Viola 'Bowles' Black'

A useful plant for adding touches of distinction to small displays. **Cultivation** It is a short-lived plant and best treated as an annual or biennial. For continuous flowering it is important not to let it set seed and to deadhead regularly. Prone to attacks by aphids, which distort and stunt the growth. Mildew is sometimes a problem. Sun. **Hardiness** Zones 4–8.

See page 46, 62

index

Acknowledgments

The author would like to give special thanks to Robin, Bella, and John for their relentless efforts through a blisteringly hot summer. Special thanks also to Craig Knowles and his very able assistants. We had a good summer. A big thanks to the whole team at Whichford Pottery and to the ever-helpful and enthusiastic ladies at Fibrex Nurseries. Many thanks all.

The publishers would like to thank Roger Hughes at Stonemarket Ltd. for all the paving and edging materials that enabled us to build our elaborate outdoor stages. To Samantha Dawe at The Think Tank for coordinating delivery of Formica finishes. To Robert Norris at Thatch International Ltd for the willow screening and wattle hurdles. We would also like to thank everyone who supplied us with containers, including Adam Caplin for the loan of his teak planter, and everyone at Evergreen, Covent Garden Flower Market.